THE BATTLE

THE
BATTLE

DEFEATING
the
ENEMIES
of
YOUR SOUL

Thomas E. Trask & Wayde I. Goodall

ZondervanPublishingHouse
Grand Rapids, Michigan

A Division of HarperCollinsPublishers

The Battle
Copyright © 1997 by Thomas E. Trask and Wayde I. Goodall

Also published in Spanish by Vida Publishers, ISBN: 0-829-71515-0

Requests for information should be addressed to:

ZondervanPublishingHouse
Grand Rapids, Michigan 49530

Library of Congress Cataloging-in-Publication Data

Trask, Thomas E.
    The battle : defeating the enemies of your soul / Thomas E. Trask and
Wayde I. Goodall.
       p. cm.
    Includes bibliographical references.
    ISBN: 0-310-21456-4 (pbk.)
    1. Spiritual warfare. 2. Spiritual life—Christianity. I. Goodall, Wayde I. II.
Title.
BT981.T73 1997
235'.5—dc21
                                      97-00000
                                         CIP

Permissions granted for use of published materials are indicated in the endnotes
on pages 223–34, which hereby become part of this copyright page.

Interior design by Sherri L. Hoffman

Printed in the United States of America

97 98 99 00 01 02 03 04 /❖ DH/ 10 9 8 7 6 5 4 3 2 1

Contents +

PART ONE

OUR POWERFUL ADVERSARY

ONE ✝

The Enemy of Our Souls

Even though the young man was the leader of the coven of witches, he didn't believe Satan or his demons would ever possess him. He thought he could play with the occult without fear of danger.

One night as he tried to sleep, he saw horrible, demonic faces swirling on the ceiling of his bedroom and leering down at him. They began to gather like a cloud and soon formed a funnel. The young man realized they were about to come into his heart![1]

He felt paralyzed in his bed. Panic overwhelmed him. He remembered that when he was a small boy he loved Jesus. He even went to the woods behind his house and pretended that he was a preacher of the gospel. The memory stirred the thought, "I'll cry out to Jesus." He forced the words out: "In Jesus' name, go!" And the demons vanished.

The next night was worse. Even more demonic forces seemed to be present. As he tried to sleep, he heard a roaring sound. When he looked up, the whole room was full of ugly, horrible creatures. Again, they formed a funnel. This time, the young man stood on his bed and shouted, "I claim the blood of Jesus!" Once again, the demons fled.

The young man knew it would get worse and soon he would not be able to withstand what was happening to him. He understood that his life was not one that would be pleasing to God. He now knew that he was toying with something that could harm and possess him. The young man called a Christian he knew and asked him to attend a crusade meeting that he had heard of.

As David Wilkerson preached, the young witch felt convicted by the Holy Spirit and surrendered his life to Christ. The next night he brought a suitcase of demon paraphernalia to the meeting. He testified that his family had had a background in the occult. Now he was free from it. He proclaimed that the occult is not a game, that Satan is very much alive and real, that spiritual warfare is a lifelong battle.

To some, "Satan" is a fictional name created a long time ago to depict evil. To others, Satan is seen in every hurtful experience—fear, sickness, tragedy, and abuse. Many have read about Satan in the Bible but have little understanding about him or what to do to avoid an onslaught. C. S. Lewis said, "There are two equal and opposite errors into which our race can fall about the devils. One is to disbelieve in their existence. The other is to believe, and to feel an excessive and unhealthy interest in them. They themselves are equally pleased by both errors."[2]

J. I. Packer has said something similar:

> On one hand, we can take Satan too seriously, as some in the early church and the Middle Ages did. This will cause us to fall out of the peace of God into morbid fears and fancies ... and we shall take up a negative view of the Christian life as primarily a course of devil-dodging exercises and anti-Satanic maneuvers.... On the other hand, we can err by not taking the devil seriously enough.... Unwillingness to take the devil seriously has two bad effects; it fools men, by keeping them from the knowledge of their danger as objects of the devil's attacks, and it dishonors Christ by robbing the cross of its significance as a conquest of Satan and his hosts.[3]

There is much naïveté about this being called Satan, yet there is no question that the Scripture clearly asserts his existence and defines his character. The Bible calls Satan the "father of lies." He is a subtle deceiver who will do anything he can to keep people from a personal experience with Christ.

Beginning with Adam and Eve, Satan has endeavored to distract people from taking God seriously and trusting in his goodness. Satan does not show up in our lives in obvious ways like the cartoon character that depicts him in a red suit with a pitch fork and tail—nor does he introduce himself as the devil, who has been a murderer from the beginning. Satan's character is subtle and manipulative, and he is better at deception than any other being. He has made this his vocation for thousands of years.

Helmut Thielicke speaks of Satan's deception of Eve in this way:

> The overture of this dialogue is thoroughly pious, and the serpent introduces himself as a completely serious and religious beast. He does not say: "I am an atheistic monster and now I am going to take your paradise, your innocence and loyalty, and turn it all upside down." Instead he says, "Children, today we're going to talk about religion, we're going to discuss the ultimate things."
>
> ... the Tempter always operates in disguise. He hides behind a mask of harmless indeed pious benevolence. All temptations in life begin in sugared form.[4]

Beware of Lions

THE SCRIPTURE TELLS US a great deal about how and why Satan wants to invade people's lives. We are important to God. Everyone has been created by God to have a relationship with Him. We have incredible potential as children of God, and the enemy of our souls knows that. What is precious to God is a mark for Satan. The eye of God is on our lives, with the intention to bless us. The eye of Satan is also on our lives, except that he wants to destroy us and our God-given potential.

Simon Peter was a man who loved to fish. He fished for his livelihood and for his leisure. He understood that fish are caught in many different ways. Sometimes fishermen will try a different time of the day or another location. One bait will work well today but won't cause the fish to turn their heads the next day. Some fish run in schools, and some fish are loners. Simon had fish figured out. Anyone who feeds his family by catching fish has to know his occupation.

Jesus saw something in Simon besides his career choice. In fact, Jesus changed Simon's name to Peter, which means "rock." Perhaps it was Peter's persistence that prompted the change, or his ability to find new ways to catch fish. It might have been his work ethic. Most certainly, Jesus saw Simon's hungry heart. Professional fishermen often work long hours and endure sleepless nights because they are unwilling to give up. Simon had little education, and he was not very goal oriented, besides taking care of the needs of his family. But he and his brother, Andrew, were good at that.

"'Come, follow me,' Jesus said, 'and I will make you fishers of men'" (Matt. 4:19). Immediately Simon and his brother changed occupations. With even more diligence they would learn how to "catch" people who needed to know Christ.

Satan saw something in Simon as well. Jesus warned Simon that Satan wanted to sift him as wheat (Luke 22:31). Satan wanted to strain or filter him out. He wanted to wear Simon down, weaken him, and burn him out. Simon's enemy actually asked God for permission to attack him.

Jesus told Simon of Satan's desire and added, "I have prayed for you, Simon, that your faith may not fail" (Luke 22:32). At that time, Simon had nary an inkling of Satan's tactics or abilities. But Simon grew in his understanding of Satan and developed his spiritual insight to a point where he became keenly aware of the enemy's tactics. Simon Peter wrote to the early church, "Be self-controlled and alert. Your enemy the devil prowls around like a roaring lion looking for someone to devour" (1 Peter 5:8).

It is interesting that Peter compared the devil to a lion. Lions prey on the weak, the wounded, the naïve, and the innocent. When they are hungry, whatever flesh is easiest to get to becomes their dinner. Mike Taliaferro, a pastor in South Africa, writes in his book *The Lion Never Sleeps*,

I have seen lions hunting. They are territorial and will not follow the migrating herds. Rather, they hunt a specific area. When a herd moves near their region, they will approach slowly. They are keenly aware of wind direction and know how to stay downwind from their prey. But often they don't care if the herd is alerted—such is their confidence.

Frequently the lion will run at a herd. Not sprinting but just jogging, the lion will frighten the herd. His aim is to get them to move. He wants to see them run. To the human eye, the herd's retreat seems normal enough. To the lion's sharp eye, dinner becomes very obvious. He notices who is old, who is tired or who is injured. A slight limp or any mannerism imperceptible to the human eye is obvious to the lion. He frightens the herd in order to spot the weak ones. Once he decides on his target, he will run past the others to get to his chosen prey.[5]

Peter informs us that an invisible, camouflaged being is hunting for Christians to devour. Satan and his demons constantly keep looking for those who are weak in their faith and trying to control those without faith. Satan never plays fair. He could care less about ethics, feelings, or the tactics he uses to trap his prey. He is an expert at guerrilla warfare, and he will be the sniper that will shoot when we least expect it. The devil doesn't care whether people believe in him; indeed, he might be able to deceive people with greater ease if they do not.

In his classic book *Screwtape Letters*, C. S. Lewis writes:

My Dear Wormwood,

I wonder you should ask me whether it is essential to keep the patient in ignorance of your own existence. That question, at least for the present phase of the struggle, has been answered for us by the High Command. Our policy, for the moment, is to conceal ourselves. Of course this has not always been so. We are really faced with a cruel dilemma. When the humans disbelieve in our existence we lose all the pleasing results of direct terrorism and we make no magicians. On the other hand, when they believe in us, we cannot make them materialists and skeptics. At least, not yet. I have great hopes that we shall learn in due time how to emotion-alize and mythologize their science to such an extent that what is, in effect, a belief in us (though not under that name), will creep in while the human mind remains closed to belief in the Enemy. The "Life Force," the worship of sex, and some aspects of Psychoanalysis may here prove useful. If once we can produce our perfect work—the Materialist Magician, the man, not using, but veritably worshipping, what he vaguely calls "Forces" while denying the existence of "spirits"—then the end of the war will be in sight. But in the meantime we must obey our orders. I do not think you will have much difficulty in keeping the patient in the dark. The fact that "devils" are predominantly comic figures in the modern imagination will help you. If any faint suspicion of your existence begins to arise in his mind, suggest to him a picture of something in red tights, and persuade him that since he cannot believe in that (it is an old text book method of confusing them) he therefore cannot believe in you.[6]

Satan only wants to control, to tear people apart, and to satisfy his hunger by blinding people to prevent them from having faith in God. His deceptive, dark, evil world operates by a different set of rules from those of our righteous, merciful God. Satan's goal is to "steal, and kill and destroy," whereas Jesus said, "I have come that they may have life, and have it to the full" (John 10:10).

One day while I was working at my desk, I received a phone call from a woman in our community who sounded very upset. She was fearful that her teenage sister might take her own life. This woman, whom I will call Becky, explained, "Karen is so anx-ious that she can't eat, sleep, or sit still. Often she talks about killing herself in order to get some peace."

I asked, "Becky, how long has Karen been feeling this way?"

She said, "I began to notice this kind of behavior about a year ago."

I immediately thought that Karen was struggling with some kind of depression or anxiety disorder. Several Christian professionals in our community came to mind to whom I could refer Karen for help. Then Becky said, "Karen has been involved in some kind of occultic activity for a couple of years."

I responded, "What kind of activity are you talking about?"

Becky explained that Karen had used a Ouija board and was consulting a witch over the telephone whenever she had problems or concerns. Karen had also experimented with communicating with "the spirit world" because the witch had promised that she would receive power and insight in doing so. Karen had developed a dependence on this paranormal telephone counselor, and the phone calls seemed to calm her down temporarily. But when the torment became more intense, Karen began crying out for help elsewhere.

As Becky talked, I began to wonder whether there was demonic activity in Karen's life. At my invitation, Becky brought Karen to my office a couple of hours later.

Becky was a neatly dressed woman in her early twenties who politely introduced herself, explaining that she attended our church occasionally. Then she introduced her sister.

Karen looked like a frightened child. Her face was pale, her eyes full of fear. She was unable to speak except to say yes or no in a very weak voice. Realizing that Karen would not be able to tell her story, I asked Becky to relate the problems once again. In greater detail this time, Becky described Karen's emotional state and her involvement in the occult.

While Becky was speaking, Karen seemed to stare right through the door of my office. She was emotionless, lethargic, and silent. When Becky finished speaking, I said, "Karen, I believe that I can offer you some help. Would you like that?"

Karen responded, "Yes, I need you to help me."

I stood up and moved to Karen. Her eyes appeared full of fear as I knelt down next to her chair. I said, "Karen, I want to pray for you right now before I offer you any counsel. Would you permit me to do that?" She nodded her head. I stated that I would pray in the name of Jesus, as He was ready to help her if she wanted Him to.

Suddenly she emitted a blood curdling scream: "Ahhh!!"

I was shocked that when I mentioned the name of Jesus, Karen screamed. Chills went up and down my spine, and I was so startled that I didn't know how to respond. Becky sat stunned and looked hopelessly at her little sister. The secretaries in the outer office reported later that the sound had frightened them. They thought someone was hurt.

It was a horrified scream, as if Karen had seen the most frightening thing she could imagine.

I regained my composure and said, "Karen, can you say, 'Jesus is Lord'?" She didn't respond. I said, "Karen, can you say, 'Jesus help me'?"

With her eyes closed, she whispered, "Jesus, help me."

I then told Karen, "I am going to pray for you. Father, in the name of Jesus I come to You, asking You to set Karen free from any demonic activity or control. By the authority of Your Son, Jesus Christ, I command the devil to set Karen free! Amen!"

Karen opened her eyes. Her face looked calm and even had a small smile. She turned her face and looked into my eyes for the first time.

"Karen, do you feel any different?" I asked.

"I do. What did you do?"

"Jesus has helped you with your problem," I explained, "and we should thank Him for freeing you from your fear. Now it is important that you stop your involvement with any occultic activity and give your life to Jesus Christ. Karen, will you give your life to Jesus?"

Karen knew that Jesus had helped her, and she said, "Yes, I want Jesus in my life."

Becky was amazed at what was going on. She was feeling both grateful and confused.

Karen unconditionally gave her life to Christ that day. She began attending our church faithfully and a few years later met a young Christian man and married him. Today this couple has two beautiful children. Karen was once a blinded victim of the devil; now she is a beautiful Christian wife and mother. She has no doubts that Jesus set her free. On that day in my office she walked away from all occultic practices and began serving the Lord, who set her free from the roaring lion. There is no question in Karen's mind that Satan is real and that Jesus Christ is the answer to his attack.

Fighting for Control

THE EFFECTS OF SATAN'S work are evident in various degrees in every country, city, town, and home on this planet. He is the creator of all evil, the father of lies, the master of deception and intrigue, and the originator of suffering. Through his demonic hosts he does all he can to keep people from acknowledging and serving the creator God. John Milton wrote,

> The infernal serpent; he it was, whose guile,
> Stirred up with envy and revenge, deceived
> The mother of mankind.[7]

Since the time of his catastrophic rebellion in heaven, Satan has progressively devised and implemented ways to influence, injure, and control God's most precious creation—people. In his unique, sick way the devil will try virtually anything to persuade a human being to choose to serve him (or anything) rather than God. His techniques are numerous, and he works endlessly, restlessly, overseeing his battle strategy to control the people of this earth. As time goes on and the day approaches when Jesus Christ will return, Satan is stepping up his activity. He knows his time is short, and he is aware that he will once again confront his creator.

The reality of Satan is not proved just by sensational stories that human imaginations have thought up. Rather, Scripture reveals his existence and defines his personality. We find him both in the Old Testament and the New Testament. As mentioned earlier, he first shows up in the Bible as the serpent that deceived Eve into disobeying God (Gen. 3:15). Satan is found in the book of Job, when he actually asked God for permission to assault the righteous man named Job (Job 2). He tempted and persuaded David to disobey God by causing him to take a census of the

Israelite community (1 Chron. 21:2). Zechariah records how Satan opposed Joshua the high priest: "Then he showed me Joshua the high priest standing before the angel of the LORD, and Satan standing at his right side to accuse him" (Zech. 3:1). Isaiah describes how Satan, who was originally named Lucifer ("daystar"), fell from the original position that God had created for him (Isa. 14:12–17). Ezekiel gives us insight about his original state and his subsequent fall (Ezek. 28:11–19). The prophet recounts, "You were blameless in your ways from the day you were created till wickedness was found in you" (v. 15). "Your heart became proud on account of your beauty" (v. 17). "You have come to a horrible end" (v. 19).

All the New Testament writers make reference to Satan, and he is referred to in nineteen of the twenty-seven books. Jesus Christ himself speaks of him twenty-five times. The gospel writers—Matthew, Mark, Luke, and John—speak descriptively of Satan's various activities.

So the Bible clearly reveals that there is an unseen spiritual being called Satan. It is critical that we understand that the Satan of the Bible is alive and well today. He has a strategy to control this world, and you are a part of his overall plan.

In his book *Demons in the World Today*, the late Merrill F. Unger writes that

> the history of various religions from the earliest times shows belief in Satan and demons to be universal. According to the Bible, degeneration from monotheism resulted in the blinding of men by Satan and the most degrading forms of idolatry (Rom. 1:21–32; 2 Cor. 4:4). By the time of Abraham (c. 2000 B.C.), men had sunk into a crass polytheism that swarmed with evil spirits. Spells, incantations, magical texts, exorcisms, and various forms of demonological phenomena abound in archeological discoveries from Samaria and Babylon. Egyptian, Assyrian, Chaldean, Greek, and Roman antiquity are rich in demonic phenomena. The deities worshipped were invisible demons represented by material idols and images.[8]

Unger then states that "early Christianity rescued its converts from the shackles of Satan and demons" (Eph. 2:2; Col. 1:13). To an amazing degree, the history of religion is an account of demon-controlled religion, particularly in its clash with the Hebrew faith and later with Christianity.[9]

The Great Rebellion

TWO PASSAGES OF SCRIPTURE help us understand where Satan came from and why he is the way he is. Isaiah 14:12–14 and Ezekiel 28:12–15 describe the fall of an angel named Lucifer, and it is clear that this angel is Satan.

Why did God create Lucifer? What caused Lucifer's fall? Why would countless other created angels decide to follow Lucifer?

We can only imagine how rebellion and sin could originate in the sinless kingdom of God. What persuaded sinless angels to rebel against a perfect, merciful, and holy God? What made them think they could be better off following the one who thought himself to be as powerful as the creator God? The deception that persuaded them to even think of opposing God is beyond comprehension. We can only assume that the timing of Lucifer's revolt was sometime after the birth of creation and his appearance in the Garden of Eden (Gen. 3).

The poet Dante reckoned that the fall of the rebellious angels took place within twenty seconds of their creation and originated in the pride that made Lucifer unwilling to await the time when he would have perfect knowledge. Others, such as Milton, put the angelic creation and fall immediately prior to the temptation of Adam and Eve in the Garden of Eden.[10] It would seem that a considerable amount of time would need to pass since creation before Lucifer could think through such a plan and, in turn, persuade a host of angels to follow his lead. The Bible does not try to explain in detail how or exactly when Satan's rebellion occurred; we only know that it did happen. There was a rebellion, a judgment, and a banishment from heaven.

Ezekiel 28 relates that Lucifer was a created angel who had incredible gifts and was perhaps one of the most powerful and talented angels of all. In describing Lucifer's original state, Ezekiel writes,

> "You were the model of perfection,
>   full of wisdom and perfect in beauty.
> You were in Eden,
>   the garden of God;...
> You were anointed as a guardian cherub,
>   for so I ordained you.
> You were on the holy mount of God;
>   you walked among the fiery stones.
> You were blameless in your ways
>   from the day you were created
>   till wickedness was found in you" (vv. 12–15).

From this passage we know that God gave this cherub angel wonderful gifts of wisdom and power. This being was created to be "perfect in beauty" and had the freedom to go to and fro in God's flawless kingdom. He might have been the wisest and most beautiful of all God's created beings who was originally placed in a position of authority over the other cherubim surrounding the throne of God.[11] Cherubim are

> of the highest order or class, created with indescribable powers and beauty.... their main purpose and activity might be summarized in this way: they are proclaimers and protectors of God's glorious presence, His sovereignty, and His holiness.[12]

Lucifer was to oversee the heavenly realm and ensure that God's presence, holiness, and sovereignty were constantly declared and defended. Instead, he did the unthinkable. He took advantage of the God who created him and thought that he could be as perfect as the Creator. What he was to protect his God from, he became a self-inflicted victim of. Isaiah gives some description of how this transpired.

You said in your heart,
  "I will ascend to heaven;
I will raise my throne
  above the stars of God;
I will sit enthroned on the mount of assembly,
  on the utmost heights of the sacred mountain.
I will ascend above the tops of the clouds;
  I will make myself like the Most High" (Isa. 14:13–14).

Pride entered Lucifer's heart, and he thought he could be as good as God. The five "I wills" became his ruin and will cause his eventual demise.

Lucifer's great responsibility and the respect he must have drawn give us a hint as to why a multitude of angels rebelled against God and His perfect kingdom. The influences of sin are contagious. Paul refers to the "secret power [hidden truth] of lawlessness" (2 Thess. 2:7). Peter informs us that "God did not spare angels when they sinned, but sent them to hell, putting them into gloomy dungeons to be held for judgment" (2 Peter 2:4). Jude 6 speaks of "the angels who did not keep their positions of authority but abandoned their own home. . . ."

Lucifer must have meditated on his tremendous abilities and beauty because he permitted himself to think that he could be *as* the One who created him. He expressed and demonstrated this attitude to numerous other angels, and they accepted it. Because of his high position—perhaps second only to God Himself—many came to the conclusion that he had something to say on the subject of "Who is the greatest?" Pride had entered those angels' hearts just as it had Satan's.

Pride is possibly the most wicked of all sins. It was through pride that Lucifer fell, and it was through pride that a multitude of angels decided to listen to and follow him. C. S. Lewis goes so far as to say, "The essential sin, the utmost evil, is Pride. Unchastity, anger, greed, drunkenness, and all that are mere fleabites in comparison: it was through Pride that the devil became the devil."[13] Lucifer became proud of his beauty and abilities. His wisdom became corrupt (Ezek. 28:17). He did not feel that God's will was good enough. He wanted to be like the "Most High."

At that time the original "war" began in heaven. Lucifer started a battle that has continued to this day. His war on this earth is the fight for the souls of mankind. Because of his mutiny he was thrown from heaven. He was no match for the "Most High," then or now, nor will he be so in the future. But Satan does not believe he will ultimately lose. The "father of lies" has been deceived by his own lies.

Although self-deception on such a grand scale seems unthinkable, Satan constantly seeks to persuade mankind to oppose God as well.

We are not told exactly how many angels decided to follow Satan's lead. Perhaps a third of them. Scripture sometimes refers to angels as stars. This explains why, prior to his fall, Satan was called the "star of the morning." The apostle John enlarges the metaphor: "His tail swept a third of the stars out of the sky and flung them to the earth" (Rev. 12:4).[14] The apostle Paul calls Satan "the ruler of the kingdom of the air, the spirit who is now at work in those who are disobedient" (Eph. 2:2). Paul further explains that our struggle is not limited to what we can see, hear, or touch: "For our struggle is not against flesh and blood, but against the rulers, against the authorities, against the powers of this dark world and against the spiritual forces of evil in the heavenly realms" (Eph. 6:12).

The war that began in heaven has spread to Earth. God's people are in a battle, and the more they advance God's kingdom, the more intense the battle becomes. The world wars, civil wars, and continuing threats of war are "little league" compared with the "major league" battle that is being fought in the unseen, spiritual world.

This battle rages continually. When Christians pray, Satan's forces try to discourage and bring doubt. When God's people plan and implement ways to bring more people to Christ, the enemy does all he can to stop or slow down the process. When angels carry out the directives of God, Satan's angels are infuriated, and they attack.

Satan is also on the offensive. He can be seen trying to deceive the "curious" through psychic hot lines, Hollywood movies and videos, television programs, and other conditions in the media. Malcom Muggeridge said, "The media have, indeed, provided the devil with perhaps the greatest opportunity accorded him since Adam and Eve were turned out of the Garden of Eden."[15]

The devil's battle plan can be subtle and very difficult to detect, although at times it becomes obvious, as in satanic worship. This enemy will attack at any location and at any time, and he will use whomever he can to persuade people to follow him. Billy Graham said, "Satan has great power. He is cunning and clever, having set himself against God and His people. He will do everything in his power to hold people captive in sin and to drag them down to the prison of eternal separation from God."[16]

Disobedience and rebellion toward God originated with Lucifer and his angels. He has devised countless unique plans to persuade people to follow his lead. But even though he has great God-given gifts and understands human behavior better than any psychologist, he cannot have power over Christians. John writes, "You, dear children, are from God and have overcome them, because the one who is in you is greater than the one who is in the world" (1 John 4:4).

Nothing to Fear

A FRIEND, JOHN BUENO, who was the pastor of a church in El Salvador, tells of an incredible experience. The church had grown to several thousand people. The sanctuary seats about two thousand people. When the Sunday service reached capacity, a second service was added, then a third and a fourth.

Returning from a trip late one Wednesday afternoon, John was tired and decided to stay home from the midweek service to get some much-needed rest. A deacon in his church called and said, "Pastor, you had better come to church tonight. A person needs deliverance. I believe he is demon possessed."

John decided that he had better attend the service after all. He relates, "I kept looking around for something strange to happen or some weird person, but I didn't see anything unusual. After the service the deacon brought the so-called demon-possessed man to me. When the man saw me, he rushed at me to attack me. I had never had this kind of experience before. The deacons held him back by gripping his arms and shoulders. I instructed them, 'Let him go. God will protect me.'"

The man had a wild look in his eyes and once again rushed at me. I shouted, "I rebuke you in the name of Jesus!" To my surprise, the man fell to the floor. We gathered around him and began praying for him. It seemed as if we were there for hours but it was really only a short time. As the man lay there, he said over and over again, "Jesus, you *are* stronger. Jesus, you *are* stronger." John then was able to communicate with the troubled man and introduce him to Jesus Christ.

Jesus is stronger! He is the creator God. Just talking about Satan can cause many to fear, but as Christians we have *nothing* to fear. "The reason the Son of God appeared was to destroy the devil's work" (1 John 3:8). This fallen angel named Satan is a roaring lion. He is hungry and determined, looking for the weak, the unprepared, the naïve, the arrogant—anyone he can devour. But Jesus Christ has defeated him and has given Christians protection from his attacks.

Two

Unmasking the Evil One

In the fall of 1989 millions of Americans were stunned when they viewed a *20/20* broadcast on television. The newscaster took viewers into numerous orphanages in Romania where tens of thousands of children, from infancy through late teens, were living in deplorable conditions. We saw rusted cribs with as many as four babies lying in them. We saw the filthy conditions and heard the empty crying of innocent children. I can't remember if my wife and I had any conversation other than an occasional gasp. We felt overwhelmed, disgusted, and helpless. When the program ended, we turned off the television set and went to bed for a restless night.

As I was driving to my office early the next morning, I felt tremendous sorrow for these orphaned children. I began to weep, so much so that I needed to pull my car over to the side of the road. I began to pray, "God, show me what to do. Please, God, show me what to do!" I added, "If there is anything I can do, please feel free to ask me and I will obey you." After I regained my composure, I continued on to the office.

Little did I know how God would take me up on my prayer. Later that day one of the church leaders called me and said, "Pastor, several of the board members saw the *20/20* broadcast last night, and we were wondering if our church could do anything at all to help these children in Romania? If you feel like you can, we want you to do whatever you think would be helpful and involve the church as much as you want." I began to inquire of the airlines how to fly to Romania.

Nicolae Ceausescu, the evil dictator of Romania for nearly twenty-five years, had died only a few months earlier. The country was in confusion, and I knew that getting into the orphanages would be difficult. However, I had to see firsthand what these children were going through.

Word spread through our community that a pastor was going to visit Romania on a fact-finding mission. The newspaper picked up the story and came by our church to do an interview. Within days, SAS Airlines called my office to inform me that someone in upper management had issued me a round-trip ticket to Vienna, Austria. When I asked who gave the ticket, the staff member only said, "Someone who is interested in what you are doing." In about six weeks I was on my way to the orphanages.

After renting a rusted-out four-wheel-drive vehicle with a Romanian driver, my two companions and I began to find our way to the orphanages. I'll never forget what I saw, heard, touched, and smelled. It was true that as many as four babies shared one rusty crib from which the paint chips fell on the urine-soaked mattress. Many small children had hollow eyes and had bones protruding from their hands, feet, legs, and face. I listened to the constant moaning of children in the background as I went from room to room. Adolescent children, who were nearly naked and were going through puberty, were freely moving from room to room. In numerous places I saw body elimination on the floor. Countless children were suffering from AIDS because needles were being used dozens of times to give inoculations.

I tried to touch some of the children, but they ran from me, afraid of a stranger. I decided to try to pick up small children who might let me to show a little love. Many were wet from urine, and their wet clothing soaked through my clothing to my skin. Their clothes were encrusted with filth. (When I returned home, my wife and the dry cleaner tried—often in vain—to get the stains out of my clothes.)

I know that the orphanage workers and nurses were trying their best, but they were radically understaffed to do this horrifying job. They didn't have enough food, medicine, clothing, cleaning supplies, or personnel to care for the children properly. They worked hard, but couldn't keep up with the enormous need. Tears of hope came to the eyes of many of the workers when they saw Americans. They hoped that we could help.

We did help as much as we could. Within months we helped six children to get adopted into American homes. We helped fund a new Christian medical clinic—a dream come true for a certain Romanian Christian pediatrician. We shipped an ambulance to this medical clinic and were able to get many thousands of dollars of medical supplies and vitamins into the country. Yet this effort was only a small splash in a very large ocean of deprivation.[1]

As the evil dictators of Romania, Ceausescu and his wife organized and approved the abuse of hundreds of thousands of children. They viewed educated people as a threat, so they simply eliminated many of them. Many of the terrible crimes against the people of Romania are on record, but only God knows the full scope of this iniquity. We do not know why this evil couple thought they needed to treat the innocent as they did. We only know that they were void of compassion and full of pride, arrogance, and destruction.

The Destroyer

HISTORY RECORDS THAT TYRANTS such as Ceausescu, Hitler, Stalin, and countless others have destroyed millions of people. "Ethnic cleansing" in Bosnia, Somalia, and wartime Germany is born out of the terrible idea that certain groups of innocent people are unneeded and unworthy and should therefore be eliminated, or at least contained. A wicked, hateful force from within drives evil dictators in their behavior.

Where does this poisonous stimulation come from? Since the time when Cain murdered his innocent brother, Abel, the "destroyer" has been actively planting evil thoughts in human beings. The abuse of children, racial or ethnic groups, Christians and other religious zealots, and countless other innocent people arises from the heart of this evil being called Satan. The fact remains that Satan still believes that he will acquire God's throne and His authority. He seeks out the rulers, potentates, chieftains, and any other human beings he can effectively empower and control to implement his evil strategy. He wanted to be the Caesar, the Hitler, and the Ceausescu of the entire universe.

The Bible reveals that one day soon, there will be a man whom Satan will possess. He is called the Antichrist, the "lawless one," and he will influence the entire world for a few years during a period known as the Great Tribulation. But this attempt of Satan's will be squelched. Paul writes that "the lawless one will be revealed, whom the Lord will overthrow with the breath of his mouth and destroy by the splendor of his coming" (2 Thess. 2:8).

Satan never plays fair but is a deceiver and a liar. He does not like you or me, and it might surprise you that he has a plan of destruction for your life. The only hope for people is to know the true and living God. Jesus came to destroy the works of the devil. To the Christian, John says, "The one who is in you is greater than the one who is in the world" (1 John 4:4).

In his book *Angels*, Billy Graham writes, "Isaiah 13:12–14 clearly points up Satan's objectives. He works to bring about the downfall of nations, to corrupt moral standards and to waste human resources. Corrupting society's order, he wants to prevent the attainment of order, and to shake the kingdoms of our God. He uses his destructive power to create havoc, fire, flood, earthquake, storm, pestilence, disease and the devastation of peoples and nations."[2] Satan is a destroyer and "the angel of the Abyss [bottomless pit], whose name in Hebrew is Abaddon, but in Greek, Apollyon" (Rev. 9:11). *Abaddon* means destruction, and *Apollyon* means destroyer. One of Satan's goals is to destroy God's creation, and he often achieves this by spiritually blinding people or eliminating them altogether. Satan's motives are never right, and his tactics are always mixed with deceit and evil intent. He is a master of intrigue and will trick anyone he can into doing his bidding.

The Opposer

THE BIBLE USES MANY other words besides "destroyer" to portray Satan. The word *Satan* itself means adversary or opposer. No less than fifty-six times the Scriptures describe Satan as the adversary of God and man. For example, Paul said that "Satan stopped" him from going to the Thessalonian church (1 Thess. 2:18).

From the time that he decided to resist God in heaven, Satan has stood in opposition to God on this earth. Erwin W. Lutzer said, "No matter how many pleasures Satan offers you, his ultimate intention is to ruin you. Your destruction is his highest priority."[3] Satan's resistance to God's ways in heaven has become resistance to God's ways on this earth. When we try to do something good for Christ or His kingdom, we can anticipate that "the adversary" will try to hinder us. This is one of his primary ways to discourage people from obeying God or doing God's will. But though he will continue to resist our attempts to do the will of God, we will not be overcome. Hermas, the writer of *The Shepherd* (c. 155), said, "The devil cannot lord it over those who are servants of God with their whole heart and who place their hope in him. The devil can wrestle with but not overcome them."[4]

The Accuser

"THE DEVIL" IS ANOTHER common term used to describe this being. The Greek word for devil, *diabolos,* means slanderer or malignant accuser. The New Testament uses this word thirty-five times. In the Scriptures we see the devil slandering and accusing Job (Job 1–2), Joshua the high priest (Zech. 3:1), and Christians in general: "For the accuser of our brothers, who accuses them before our God day and night . . ." (Rev. 12:10). The devil tempted

Jesus in the wilderness when he was praying for forty days; he tempted Adam and Eve in the garden; and he tries to accuse and slander people today. The devil is pleased when he can reproduce his character in people by influencing them to malign others. He especially likes to get Christians to act this way because such behavior will bring disunity to the church and enable non-Christians to say that Christians aren't any different from anyone else. The result is that many people could decide not to come to Christ because of the behavior they observe in some of His people.

The One Who Corrupts

SATAN IS ALSO CALLED Beelzebul—literally, Baalzebub—"Lord of the fly." This term is defined in Matthew 12:24: "Beelzebub, the prince of demons." He corrupts everything he touches. Martin Luther said, "I am a great enemy to flies. When I have a good book, they flock upon it and parade up and down upon it and soil it. 'Tis just the same with the devil. When our hearts are purest, he comes and soils them."[5] Satan contaminates personal life by dispensing a so-called new morality, an ethic of compromise. He damages social life by introducing drugs, drunkenness, and debauchery. He corrupts political life by promoting bribery, insincerity, and deceit. And he continually seeks to infect church life by advancing false doctrines and heresy.

There are several other ways, in fact, by which Beelzebub seeks to corrupt the church. John calls Satan "the accuser of our brothers" (Rev. 12:10). If he has opportunity, Satan will accuse Christian people to their God. He continually accuses Christians in their thoughts, whispering, "You can't be good enough for God," or he will remind them of a past sin by saying, "God will never forgive you for that." Satan can wear down children of God through persistent slanders, telling them they are not worthy of God's forgiveness or that He will always have something against them. Satan wants to rob Christians of their peace, but they can reject this thought by remembering the truth of what Jesus did for them on the cross. It is said that Satan confronted Martin Luther with a list of his sins. Luther admitted that all of the sins that Satan listed were, in fact, true. He then turned to the accuser and said, "Write this across them all. The blood of Jesus cleanses us from them all!"

The Cunning One

ONE OF THE OLDEST names used of the devil is "the serpent." It was through the serpent that Satan brought the original temptation to Eve, enticing her by questioning God's instructions. Paul warns us, "But I am afraid that just as Eve was deceived by the serpent's cunning, your minds may somehow be led astray" (2 Cor. 11:3). John writes of "that ancient serpent called the devil, or Satan, who leads the whole world astray" (Rev. 12:9). Isaiah refers to the devil as "the twisted serpent" (Isa. 27:1 NASB). Jesus used a serpent as a symbol of deceit and hypocrisy (Matt. 23:33).

Satan turns great wisdom into craftiness and evil cunning. John Milton described "the serpent—subtlest beast of all the field."[6] Somehow this creature "serpent" that approached Eve became attractive and craftily deceived her into questioning God's warning, His goodness, and His word. The serpent operates the same way today. He tries to persuade us that we can do as we please and ignore the rules. Many people claim to believe in God and even call themselves "born again," but feel they do not have to obey God. The lie hasn't changed, only the times. Helmut Thielicke said, "God put at man's disposal the whole breadth of his creation: the multitude of plants and animals are at his service, the laws of nature are there to be explored and technologically utilized, and the whole cosmos is offered as his dominion. Only one single spot in all this infinite expanse must remain taboo, inviolable, and reserved to God himself, namely, this one tree. And at this one point the serpent now begins to fire away."[7] Our commitment to complete obedience to Christ is what the serpent will try to get us to compromise.

The Murderer

SATAN IS CALLED A murderer. Jesus said that the devil has been "a murderer from the beginning" (John 8:44) and that he wants to "kill and destroy" (John 10:10). Satan invented murder and destruction. Today murder is on the increase and is epidemic in many cities. On the evening news we continually hear of murder: domestic violence, a drug killing, a drive-by shooting, or mere vengeance.

In Chicago, two young people dangled a five-year-old child out a fourteenth-story window. It was around six o'clock on a typical day at the Ida B. Wells Public Housing Project on Chicago's south side. On this October evening the fall weather had brought a bitter chill as children in the Hood struggled to stay warm.

Earlier that day A.J. and P.R. had enticed little Eric Morse to come to their clubhouse on South Langley Avenue. These boys— ages ten and eleven—were like heroes to little Eric, but they were already working for the gangs.

"Come to the fourteenth floor at number 1405, Eric. We have a surprise for you," they said. But Eric's eight-year-old brother Derrick begged him not to go. Eric refused to listen and said he was going to the clubhouse for a surprise. Derrick insisted on going with him because he didn't trust A.J. and P.R.

When Eric arrived at the apartment, A.J. and P.R. grabbed him and dangled him out the window. Derrick screamed and ran to the window and held Eric's leg as the little guy screamed in terror. While Derrick held on—trying to pull Eric back into the apartment—A.J. bit his arm, and Derrick let go. At four minutes before eight o'clock, little Eric died.[8]

The story shook countless people in Chicago and around the country. What could make these young people think that they could get away with such a wicked thing? How could they be so cruel and uncaring? "How could this happen?" you ask. There is no question that these young people committed this terrible act by their own volition—yet, the murderer prompted them. Satan is a destroyer, and he will continue to tempt people to kill and destroy until he is incarcerated in his eternal abode called Hell. Murder and destruction are his goals, and he will prey on as many people as he can.

The Deceiver

SATAN IS THE ORIGINATOR of deception and will beguile people by appearing to have good—even angelic—intentions. Tertullian, one of the church fathers, said, "The devil tries to shake truth by pretending to defend it."[9] Paul instructs that Satan can transform himself into an angel of light. He fully understands how angels operate and he often uses evil men as his agents. Some of these men have even crept into the Christian church. Paul calls these "so called" leaders "false apostles, deceitful workman, masquerading as apostles of Christ. And no wonder, for Satan himself masquerades as an angel of light" (2 Cor. 11:13, 14). Satan's attempts to distract the church or to bring disunity will be discussed in a later chapter.

The Tempter

SATAN LIKES TO TEMPT and provoke people to sin. He did this to the celestial spirits that are his demons, causing them to lose "their own domain" (Jude 6 NASB; see also Revelation 12:8), and he continues to tempt people today. He tempted Jesus (Matt. 4:3), and he continues to tempt Christians in spite of their relationship with God (1 Thess. 3:5).

The verb to tempt has two senses in the Bible. One means to test with the purpose of perfecting or developing character. God is involved in this way with every Christian because He desires that we grow in our faith. This sense is a neutral use of the word. The other sense has a negative meaning, "provoke to evil." This activity belongs entirely to Satan. We do not sin when we are tempted by Satan, but we sin when we yield to that temptation.

God wants only what is good for us; Satan wants only what will harm us. In his book *Perelandra,* C. S. Lewis portrays the way Satan tempts people:

> "Listen, Lady," said Ransom. "There is something he is not telling you. All this that we are now talking has been asked before. The thing he wants you to try has been tried before. Long ago, when our world began, there was only one man and one woman in it, as you and the King are in this. And there once before he stood, as he stands now, talking to the woman. He had found her alone as he has found you alone. And she listened, and did the thing Maleldil had forbidden her to do. But no joy and splendor came of it. What came of it I cannot tell you because you have no image of it in your mind. But all love was troubled and made cold, and Maleldil's voice became hard to hear so that wisdom grew little among them; and the woman was against the man and the mother against the child; and when they looked to eat there was no fruit on their trees, and hunting for food took all their time, so that their life became narrower, not wider."[10]

God will bring testing throughout our lives but will never be involved in any tempting us to sin. James instructs us, "When tempted, no one should say, 'God is tempting me.' For God cannot be tempted by evil, nor does he tempt anyone" (James 1:13). Satan and his demonic cohorts are continually watching for ways to tempt both unbelievers and believers to disobey God.

The Wicked One

JOHN DESCRIBES SATAN AS the evil one, or the wicked one. Jesus prayed that God the Father would protect His followers from the evil one (John 17:15), and John reminds us that "the whole world is under the control of the evil one" (1 John 5:19). Just as God is the embodiment of all that is good and holy, Satan is the embodiment of all that is evil and unholy. Satan's essential nature is evil. John Milton said that the devil is "the strongest and fiercest spirit / That fought in heaven, now fiercer by despair."[11] Satan's very nature and basic elements are unholy and despicable. He is ingrained with harmful motives and corrupt morals. He is the evil one.

The Worldly Prince

THE BIBLE DESCRIBES SATAN as the "prince of this world" (John 14:30). This "prince," or ruler, heads up the godless world system. This title is given to him because sinners grant him godlike worship and blindly hold him in reverence, as Christians do with God Himself. God's heavenly kingdom operates in absolute purity, holiness, peace, and truth. Satan's earthly kingdom is full of moral filth, apprehension, fear, and lies. He motivates people to be greedy. He tries to persuade people to atheism, believing that there is no God. Through his obedient fallen angels Satan promotes violence and wars.

Remember, these fallen creatures were once angels and have not been stripped of all their power. Whatever Satan can devise to blind a person to the truth, he will do it. He has a unique plan for every human being. This "ruler" has blinded the minds of unbelievers into following his orders for thousands of years (see 2 Corinthians 4:4). Only after a person comes to Christ will he or she begin to truly understand how God's kingdom functions.

The Ruler of the Demonic Kingdom

SATAN IS CALLED THE "ruler of the kingdom of the air" (Eph. 2:2). William Barclay explains, "It is life lived under the dictates of the prince of the air. . . . The ancient world believed strenuously in demons. They believed that the air was so crowded with these demons that there was not room to insert a pinpoint between them. Pythagoras said: 'The whole air is full of Spirits.' Philo said: 'There are spirits flying everywhere through the air.'"[12] We know that as spirit beings, angels move through the air from one place to another. Throughout this world God's obedient angels do His bidding, and Satan's obedient demonic beings do his will.

The Bible records that Daniel prayed, and in response God sent an angel with His answer. Yet the angel was detained by "the prince of the Persian kingdom" for twenty-one days. God in turn sent Michael, one of the chief angels—("princes," NIV)—to help His messenger angel (see Daniel 10:11–13). Michael was able to overcome the prince of the kingdom of Persia—a powerful demonic angel—and the messenger angel was free to bring God's response to Daniel. This battle took place in the spirit world. With our human eyes we cannot see how many demons there are nor can we see the angelic battles being fought, but we know from Scripture that this spiritual world does exist and that Satan is its temporary ruler, the "prince of the kingdom of the air."

The Master Counterfeiter

WE HAVE MENTIONED HERE only a few of the approximately thirty names the Bible uses to describe Satan. We can clearly see that Satan wants God's territory and still believes that he will rule with all the power of God Himself. St. Augustine called Satan *Simius Dei*, "the ape" or the imitator of God that comes as an angel of light. Satan is a master counterfeiter. He wants to look like the real thing. The question is often asked, "If Satan is so deceiving and can trick people so easily, what chance do I have?" We must understand that for Christians walking with God, God is their protector. If we are sincerely trying to serve Christ and be obedient to Him, we will know when the devil attempts to deceive us.

The situation is like a counterfeit bill. How can a person know the real from the fake? We have to become so acquainted with the real thing that a glance at or a feel of the fake will identify it immediately. Casual believers who do not stay in the Word and do not have a consistent fellowship with the Lord can be tricked by the enemy. They can be fooled. It will take them longer to catch on to what the devil is doing.

The enemy is a master at deception, and he will approach a believer as an angel of light. Dorothy L. Sayers wrote of Satan,

His method of working is to present us with the magnificent set-up, hoping we shall not use either our brains or our spiritual faculties to penetrate the illusion. He is playing for sympathy; therefore he is much better served by exploiting our virtues than by appealing to our lower passions; consequently, it is when the devil looks most noble and reasonable that he is most dangerous.[13]

The devil will put on camouflage and be able to deceive those who are not aware of his devices. The Scripture says that in the last days he will deceive—if that is possible—even the elect (see Matthew 24:22–24). In his desire to imitate God, Satan has developed

His own theology: "doctrines of demons" (1 Tim. 4:1 NASB)
His own ministers (2 Cor. 11:4–5)
His own church: the "synagogue of Satan" (Rev. 2:9)
His own trinity: the devil, the beast, and the false prophet (Rev. 16:13)
His own sacrificial system: "the sacrifices of pagans" (1 Cor. 10:20)
His own communion service: "the cup of demons" and "the table of demons" (1 Cor. 10:21)
His own gospel (Gal. 1:7–8)
His own throne (Rev. 13:2)
His own worshipers (Rev. 13:4)
False Christs (Matt. 24:4–5)
False teachers to bring his teachings (2 Peter 2:1)
False prophets (Matt. 24:11; 2 Peter 2:1)
False brothers (Gal. 2:4)
False apostles (2 Cor. 11:13)

Satan wants to draw people away from God and the salvation He offers. The enemy does all he can to stop or obstruct the gospel message, but his power is limited. He is not omnipotent—all powerful. This is an attribute only of God Himself. Nor is Satan omnipresent. He cannot be everywhere in his totality at the same time. Again, this quality belongs only to God. Satan also is not omniscient—all knowing. Only God knows all things actual and possible, whether past, present, or future.

The devil cannot create, but only counterfeit. He cannot know everything; he can only tempt you to think he knows everything. He cannot be everywhere at the same time, but he can assign his demonic forces to represent him in various locations. Writing in *Life* magazine, Whittaker Chambers asked the devil whether there might not be an end to his dialectics:

> The devil says: "I have brought man to the point of intellectual pride where self-extermination lies within his power. There is not only the bomb, . . . there are the much less discussed delights of bacteriological annihilation. And it is only a question of time until whole populations can be driven insane in time of war by sound which their ears cannot hear but their nerves cannot bear."
>
> "Just what do you get out of it?" asked the pessimist.
>
> "My friend," said Satan, "you do not understand the Devil's secret. But since shamelessness is part of my pathos, there is no reason why I should not tell you. The devil is sterile. I possess the will to create (hence my pride), but I am incapable of creating (hence my envy). And with an envy raised to such power as mortal minds can feel, I hate the Creator and His creation. My greatest masterpiece is never more than a perversion—an ingenious disordering of another's grand design, a perversion of order into chaos, of life into death. Why? . . . Perhaps, it is simply, as every craftsman knows, that nothing enduring, great or small, can ever be created without love. But I am as incapable of love as I am of goodness. I am as insensitive to either as a dead hand is to a needle thrust through it."[14]

Harold Lindsell said, "Satan is neither omnipotent nor free to do everything he pleases. Prince of the world he may be, but the Prince of Peace has come and dealt him a death blow."[15] This angel once had the power of death over people, but that power was broken through what Christ did for mankind on the cross: "That by his death he might destroy him who had the power of death—that is, the devil" (Heb. 2:14). Through His substitutionary death Christ defeated Satan, rendering him impotent in a believer's life.[16]

Some people reading this list of names and definitions of Satan may feel anxious and fearful of what he might do to them. We must know who Satan is and should understand his potential, but if we are Christians, we need not fear him. James tells us to "resist the devil, and he will flee from you" (James 4:7). John comforts believers by assuring us that "the one who was born of God keeps him safe, and the evil one does not touch him" (1 John 5:18). A. W. Tozer said, "Christ in you, the hope of glory. I'm not afraid of the devil. The devil can handle me—he's got judo I never heard of. But he can't handle the One to whom I'm joined; he can't handle the One to whom I'm united; he can't handle the One whose nature dwells in my nature."[17]

The only hope for anyone is to serve Christ. We cannot win the battle against the enemy of our souls in our own strength. There is no physical training, mental exercise, or emotional strength that can rebuff this wicked being when he desires to attack. There is only one way to win, and that is to have a personal relationship with Jesus Christ. When we know Christ, we have a power that the world does not have. The next step is to serve Him one day at a time—moment by moment deciding not to yield to temptation, resolving to disbelieve any accusation that the enemy might bring against us. We must continually look for the sly serpent that would cause us to question God's will and constantly be aware that the enemy of the soul will try to deceive us at any time. Then, and only then, can you and I resist him and withstand his attempts to destroy us.

Oswald Chambers said, "We cannot stand against the wiles of the devil by our wits. The devil only comes along the line that God understands, not along the lines we understand, and the only way we can be prepared for him is to do what God tells us, stand complete in his armor, indwelt by his Spirit, in complete obedience to him."[18]

THREE ✦

The Forces
of Darkness

As we walked across the office parking lot after work, I noticed a teenage boy. His eyes were intensely fixed upon us as we neared him. "How's it going?" my friend Hal asked.

"Good," the youth replied, retrieving a purple bag from his pocket, then emptying a pile of miniature tiles into his palm.

I asked, "What's that you have in your hand?"

"It's magic—white magic," he said.

The metal tiles bore occultic symbols. Hal and I promptly set down our briefcases and began inquiring about the teen's religious beliefs. He was fascinated by witchcraft and oblivious to how it conflicted with the teachings of the Bible. His name was Darrol, and he said he was seventeen, but he didn't look it. He was insecure, poorly dressed, and thin, with a large scar on his arm that made me think he had had a cut that had never been treated by a doctor. He had many bruises on his other arm and seemed somewhat frightened.

"White magic has helped me know God," he said.

I quickly explained that God doesn't need "magic" to speak to us, that we can know Him without resorting to meaningless tiles. I pulled my Bible from my briefcase and said, "Darrol, there is only one way to really know God. There is only one mediator, or ladder, between you and God. There are lots of ways people have invented to make you think there are many roads to heaven, but there is only one." I pointed to the little tiles and said, "Darrol, those tiles won't get you there. God cares much more for you than that. He gave His only son, Jesus, to die for you so that you could know God. And, Darrol, He will always be there to help you and tell you what to do."

Darrol seemed to be listening so I kept talking. "May I show you some things in this book called the Bible?"

He said, "Yes, sure, go ahead."

I presented several verses of Scripture that give the plan of salvation. Minutes later, the youth recited the "sinner's prayer" along with me.

We talked about the decision he had just made, and then I asked Darrol whether he would accept an exchange for his bag of tiles. I wanted to destroy the devil's utensils. Darrol refused to give them up, so I didn't push him. Hal and I prayed for him, gave him our office phone numbers, and watched him go on his way across the parking lot.

I really didn't think a whole lot more about this experience for the rest of the evening. But while I was at work the next morning, the switchboard operator alerted me that a young man was in the foyer and asking for me. He said he needed to talk to me. I asked the operator, "By any chance, is the young man's name Darrol?"

She said, "Well, yes, how did you know?"

"I spoke to him last night and prayed for him in our parking lot," I responded. "Please show him where the elevator is and send him up to my floor. I'll meet him when he gets off the elevator."

As Darrol sat down in my office, he looked around. "Is this where you work?"

"Yes Darrol," I said, "but for many years I worked in a church as a pastor. Doing that prepared me for what I do here." I changed the subject. "I'm glad to see you today. Over the night did you think about what we talked about yesterday."

"Yes," Darrol replied, "I thought about it a lot and wanted to give these tiles to you. I don't think I'll need them anymore."

He went on. "How did you become a minister? Maybe I could become one someday, too."

I encouraged him, saying, "Darrol, if you want to live for God, stay away from white magic and anything else that God hates. And if you love people, it could be that God would ask you to be a minister someday."

The young man said, "Don't worry, Mr. Goodall, I won't touch it again."[1]

Darrol is typical of many teenagers today: impressionable, but also mindful and curious of the supernatural. Many are looking for God in all the wrong places. Satan has created a multitude of ways to distract people from the truth. He understands that people are hungry for a spiritual experience, and he does all he can to keep people from having a relationship with Jesus Christ. He and his demonic world are busy deceiving, counterfeiting the real, and blinding people spiritually. Satan cannot be everywhere at once, but he commands his cohorts to carry out his orders around the world.

If we accept the reality of Satan's existence on the authority of the Bible and the numerous statements of Jesus Christ, then for the same reasons we must accept the reality of demons, over whom Satan rules. As we saw earlier, the angel Lucifer, was the head of myriads of angels of varying ranks. When he deceived himself into thinking that he could be as God, he was also able to persuade a multitude of angels to fall into line. Lucifer became Satan—"opposer"—and the fallen angels became demons, or evil spirits.

According to the Bible, there are two groups of fallen angels, and they reside in three places. The first group are those who are imprisoned. Some are bound in eternal confinement because of monstrous sins they have committed. Their prison is Tartarus (translated "hell" in 2 Peter 2:4). Jude 6 speaks of "the angels who did not keep their positions of authority but abandoned their own home—these he has kept in darkness, bound with everlasting chains for judgment on the great Day." W. E. Vine says that "Tartarus . . . is neither Sheol nor Hades nor Hell, but the place where those angels whose special sin is referred to in that passage (2 Pe 2:4) are confined 'to be reserved unto judgment.' The region is described as 'pits of darkness.'"[2]

Another dwelling place for fallen angels is the Pit, or the Abyss (see Luke 8:31; Revelation 9:1–2). Apparently these have been confined because of their evil potential, but the Bible indicates they will be discharged during the Tribulation and be free to torment people who are not protected by God (see Revelation 9:3–11).

The second group of fallen angels are not confined but instead are engaged in spiritual warfare at this time. This group comprises the demons. (The New Testament uses the terms *demons, unclean spirits,* and *evil spirits* interchangeably.) We do not know what percentage of the fallen angels are permanently imprisoned in Tartarus, temporarily confined to the Pit, or free to do their activity on the earth.

There is no evidence that demons are anything but fallen angels. Many theories exist to try to explain where these beings came from, why they were created, who created them, and what their original purpose was. We need to be careful to examine every theory by the Word of God to avoid unwise speculation on the subject.

Where Do Demons Come From?

IT IS HELPFUL TO review the most common theories about where demons came from.

Demons are the spirits of a pre-Adamic race. The theory of the pre-Adamic race is based on the "gap theory" of origins and suggests that there were another people created to inhabit the earth before the creation of Adam and Eve. The theory proposes that there is a gap in time between the first two verses of Genesis 1. An original creation supposedly rebelled, fell, and was destroyed. Genesis 1:3 describes a re-creation. The departed spirits of the original creation became demons.

The problem with this theory is that Romans 5:12 clearly states that sin entered into this world through Adam, not any pre-Adamic race. There is no biblical justification for this viewpoint.

Demons are the spirits of deceased evil people. Some early Christian writers and ancient Greeks held that demons are the spirits of deceased evil people. Philo and Josephus seem to have embraced this theory.

This idea is not credible because the Bible states that evil people dwell in Hades after death (Luke 16:23). We have no indication in Scripture that a spirit has the ability to freely dwell and function on the earth after the person dies. The spirits of people without Christ go to Hades, and those who belong to Jesus and have become His followers go to be with Him in heaven (2 Cor. 5:8; see also Hebrews 9:27).

Demons are the offspring of angels and women. The idea that demons are half human and half angelic is based on the proposition that evil angels had sexual relations with women and as a result produced Nephilim (Gen. 6:4) and that these Nephilim were demons (see Genesis 6:1–6).

There are many problems with this theory. The Hebrew word *Nephilim* has been variously translated as "giants" (KJV), "fallen ones" (NIV), "mighty ones," or "fierce warriors," but never "spirit beings." There is no suggestion in Scripture that demons can be reproduced or that evil angels can have sexual relations with people. Jesus taught that angels do not marry (Matt. 22:30; Mark 12:25).

Demons are the fallen but unrestrained angels that followed Satan. The view consistently propounded in Scripture is that demons are fallen angels that followed Satan. When the angel Lucifer rebelled against God, he persuaded a multitude of lower angels to do the same. As a result, they were expelled from heaven. They are now in conflict with God and His holy angels. Revelation 12:7–9 speaks of this rebellion:

> And there was war in heaven. Michael and his angels fought against the dragon, and the dragon and his angels fought back. But he was not strong enough, and they lost their place in heaven. The great dragon was hurled down—that ancient serpent called the devil, or Satan, who leads the whole world astray. He was hurled to the earth, and his angels with him.

This passage refers to Lucifer, as the "ruler of the demons" (Matt. 12:24 NASB), and his followers collectively as "the dragon and his angels." They will all eventually be condemned to "the eternal fire prepared for the devil and his angels" (Matt. 25:41).

What Are Demons Like?

Demons are personal beings. Demons are personal beings having emotions, a will, and the ability to think, speak, make decisions, and take action.

Demons have emotions. They are fearful of Jesus and his followers (Luke 8:31) and become angry and violent (Mark 9:20, 26). They are also powerful beings and can inflict physical and psychological disabilities on those who have been possessed (Mark 9:17–18; Luke 8:27–28).

The book of Acts relates an unusual incident that reveals much about the nature of demons. Seven brothers tried to conduct an exorcism, and they were surprised when the demon refused to come out of the man: "One day the evil spirit answered them, 'Jesus I know, and I know about Paul, but who are you?' Then the man who had the evil spirit jumped on them and overpowered them all" (Acts 19:15–16). These men had no authority because they did not know Jesus personally; they were merely using his name because they had observed Christian believers casting out demons. The New Testament indicates that Christians have the power to pray for people who are demon possessed and see them set free as a result (Acts 8:6–7; 16:16–18).

Demons can think and make intellectual decisions. Demons know who Christians are, as the account of the seven brothers shows. Demons are able to make decisions. The fallen angels "abandoned their own home" (Jude 6). They made a willful decision to sin (2 Peter 2:4). They are intelligent: "A man in their synagogue who was possessed by an evil spirit cried out, 'What do you want with us, Jesus of Nazareth? Have you come to destroy us? I know who you are—the Holy One of God!'" (Mark 1:23–24).

Demons do not have physical bodies. Even though they are personal beings, demons do not have physical bodies. There is no indication in Scripture that demons can take a material or tangible form. In Greek the word for *ghost* is also the word for *spirit*. These beings are spiritual and independent of matter unless they inhabit a person. After His resurrection Jesus told His disciples,

"Touch me and see; a ghost does not have flesh and bones, as you see I have" (Luke 24:39).

Demons can inhabit other creatures' bodies. Perhaps in part because they are incorporeal, demons seem to have a strong desire to inhabit, or possess, people or animals (see Mark 5:11–13) to achieve their ruler's ends. *The Concise Evangelical Dictionary of Theology* describes demon possession this way:

> The majority of references to demonic activity in the NT occur in the Synoptic Gospels and deal with confrontations between Jesus and the demon possessed. The record of Jesus' encounters with demons includes (1) physical or mental affliction—nakedness, mental anguish, and masochism (Mt. 8:28–33; Mk. 5:1–10; Lk. 8:26–39), inability to speak (Mt. 9:32; 12:22; Mk. 9:17), blindness (Mt. 12:22), and lunacy (Mt. 4:24; 17:15). (2) The demon recognizing and fearing Jesus (Mk. 11:24; 5:7; Lk. 4:34; 8:28). (3) Jesus' power over the demons is demonstrated, usually by their exorcism through the power of the word (Mt. 4:24; 8:16; Mk. 7:30) or by Jesus' permission for them to depart (Mt. 8:32; Mk. 5:13; Lk. 8:32).[3]

Merrill F. Unger offers a lengthy discussion of demon possession, but the following summary in *The Moody Handbook of Theology* describes some of its characteristics:

> Demon possession evidences itself by a change in moral character and spiritual disposition. Frequently a different voice, a different educational level, or even a foreign language will reflect a difference in the affected person's personality. The demons speaking through the man immediately recognized who Christ was (Mk. 1:23–24), which meant he had supernatural knowledge and intellectual power. Another symptom of demon possession was exhibited by the man in the country of the Gerasenes with his supernatural physical strength and ability to break shackles and chains (Mk. 5:3–4).[4]

Demons believe in God and in judgment for sin. Demons know that God exists. They know who God the Father is, they fully understand who Jesus is, and they are aware that the Holy Spirit is active in this world. "You believe that there is one God. Good! Even the demons believe that—and shudder" (James 2:19). They are terribly afraid of Jesus because they recognize His authority as God and their creator (Col. 1:16) and His ability to do whatever He pleases to them.

All demons are evil, but some are evidently more evil than others (Matt. 12:45). They are also aware that they will eventually be judged and punished: "They shouted, 'Have you come here to torture us before the appointed time?'" (Matt. 8:29; see also Matthew 25:41).

Can Christians Be Demon Possessed?

WE HAVE OBSERVED THAT demons can inhabit human beings and other creatures. So the question arises whether they can possess or inhabit Christians. Charles Ryrie offers this succinct answer:

> A demon residing in a person, exerting direct control and influence over that person, with certain derangement of mind and/or body. Demon possession is to be distinguished from demon influence or demon activity in relation to a person. The work of the demon in the latter is from the outside; in demon possession it is from within. By this definition a Christian cannot be possessed by a demon since he is indwelt by the Holy Spirit.[5]

Many Christians are confused by the suggestion that there might be demon possession or at least demonic activity in their lives. There is in fact no record in the New Testament of demons being cast out from believers, only from nonbelievers. When Christians believe that demons can possess, or have possessed, them, this can be terrifying and destructive psychologically. The experiences of dealing with so-called possessed Christians reported by demonologists simply do not conform with Scripture. Such "deliverances" may be psychologically suggested or hypnotically produced.

It is also possible that the person being prayed for, while professing to be a Christian, really is not. Many people attend church, grow up in Christian homes, and even display Christian conduct, but are not truly followers of Jesus. If these people have opened themselves up to the occult or demonic activity, possession is possible. When people permit Satan to come in and take residence in their lives, they become servants of his. Likewise, when we become Christians, we become servants of Jesus Christ. When a Christian feels overwhelmed because of demonic activity in his or her life, it means there is sin that has to be dealt with. Sin is the source of the trouble. We must distinguish between sin and demons.

The bottom line is that it is risky to interpret the Scriptures on the basis of experience. To do so is unsatisfactory, unwise, and on occasion even dangerous. Experiences may vary, but the truth of the Word of God, when rightly understood, is constant.

Even though Christians cannot be possessed, external demonic activity is possible because demons are at the disposal of Satan and he will try to do anything he can to discourage Christians or tempt them to compromise their faith. If a Christian yields to temptation and falls into sin, the enemy will do all he can to promote this behavior to become a habit.

Satan can exert influence through temptation and deceitful strategies, but he cannot direct a Christian's thoughts. If any Christians have unconfessed sin in their lives, it is important that they obey the Holy Spirit within them and repent, confess their sin, and receive God's forgiveness. Often Satan will provoke these people to self-condemnation even though in God's sight the sins have already been forgiven. But this is not possession—this is Satan and his demons seizing a moment of weakness. They want to do all they can to ruin a person's faith and testimony.

Demons know they cannot possess true Christians because Jesus Christ dwells in believers and has reclaimed them from Satan's territory. "For he has rescued us from the dominion of darkness and brought us into the kingdom of the Son he loves, in whom we have redemption, the forgiveness of sins" (Col. 1:13–14). Demons try to influence, tempt, and deceive Christians, but they can succeed only if a person is not in a right relationship with God.

Demons are quite aware of their limitations in regard to Christians. "You, dear children, are from God and have overcome them, because the one who is in you is greater than the one who is in the world" (1 John 4:4). In the Puritan classic *The Christian in Complete Armour*, William Gurnall writes, "The devil's rule is over those who are in a *state* of sin and ignorance, not over those who are sometimes sinful or ignorant. Otherwise, he would take hold of saints as well as unregenerate sinners."[6]

In the book *David Wilkerson Speaks Out*, the author states:

> The Bible makes it positively clear that he who is born of God cannot be ruled or possessed by Satan. Satan cannot possess any person who has been born of God! Demons cannot enter a bloodwashed child of Christ! Satan comes against me but has no influence, no power, no entrance—has nothing in me. It is blasphemy to believe that Satan can bind and cast out the Christ in the believer. Satan does not have access to the mind of Christ in me. Their is only one way for Satan to gain entrance and that is for a man to cast off his faith and love and turn aside, begging for trouble.[7]

People who believe that demons can dwell in the true believer do not understand the nature of salvation through Jesus Christ. That a person could be partly inhabited by the Holy Spirit and partly inhabited by demons is inconceivable from a biblical theological perspective. There is no doubt that God delivers people from various kinds of bondage instantaneously, but for a Christian to attribute foibles to the direct activity of demons is both unbiblical and psychologically harmful. Christians are protected by their heavenly Father, and they need not fear being possessed by Satan or any of his demons.

Demon Possession in Non-Christians

I[8] HAVE WITNESSED SEVERAL occurrences when people were possessed, and the effects of Satan's work are tragic. On one occasion a young woman, demon possessed, came to me, sincerely wanting me to pray for her. I could see from her eyes and her behavior that she was deeply troubled. As I and some other Christians who were there with me began to talk and pray, the demonic spirit tried to destroy her. She fell to the floor and began pounding her head on the concrete.

I quickly said, "Put a pillow under her head so she doesn't injure herself!" When the pillow was under her head, she stopped the pounding. The demon knew he could not hurt her with the pillow there. When the pillow was removed, she began hitting her head against the floor again.

"Leave the pillow there and we will pray for her right there," I said.

It was heartwrenching to see how this woman, with seemingly so much potential, wanted to take her life. She had no idea about the love of God and His power to deliver her from this horrendous desire. I knew that her main problem was demonic although there may have been a degree of psychological imbalance also.

I asked the woman, "Can you say the name of Jesus Christ, or can you say 'the blood of Jesus covers my sins'?" She could not speak these words and only responded with other words and groans.

I instructed my friends that we were going to begin praying for her again. We prayed with all the faith we could find. We quoted Scripture and used the authority that Jesus Christ had given us. Our prayers went along the lines of "In the name of Jesus Christ I command you to come out of her!"[9]

There was no immediate response, so we continued, "Satan, come out immediately! You must leave because Jesus is more powerful than you. All of us plead the blood of Jesus Christ over _____, and we demand that all demons leave!"

As we prayed, the evil spirits left the woman. Before our eyes she became normal and gained complete control over the desire to harm herself.

This experience served to remind me that people who are actually possessed have little control over their conduct. They are servants of the evil forces and the devil. The experience also reveals the incredible evil desires that Satan and his demons intend in people's lives. I am persuaded that we will see more and more demon possession in these times. With the increased interest in demons and paranormal experiences in American society, many are opening themselves up, wittingly or unwittingly, to the spirit world. Demons will take advantage of a person's interest in them. Their ultimate goal is to control a person through possession. It could be that we have as much or more demon possession today as in the times of Jesus—except that these days demons have developed sophisticated ways to control the possessed. Remember: They are subtle and deceptive, just like the one who leads them.

There is a tremendous amount of curiosity today about the occult. Nightly we see 900 psychic hotlines promoted on television; astrology, psychic phenomena, and New Age channelers are commonplace as we approach a new century. People seem to be hungry for a spiritual experience and recklessly enter into any "spiritual" activity without thinking about the consequences. One person I know hired a witch to entertain her guests at a party. This person attends church regularly, has placed her children in a private church school, and is a good citizen of her community—but she had no idea what she was doing. Her choice of entertainment could have brought spiritual disaster to her and her guests. It is a dangerous thing to play occultic games or become involved in demonic forces. It is critical that people understand the seriousness of the power of the enemy.

A Religion of the Last Days

THE NEW AGE MOVEMENT is a major attempt by Satan to distract searching people from the true God. This religion has many faces around the world and is infested with demonic activity. Hundreds of New Agers—including popular film celebrities—have moved to the northwestern part of the United States[10] to listen to ancient spirits like Ramtha, supposedly a thirty-thousand-year-old warrior who speaks through J. Z. Knight of Yelm, Washington. Two-thousand-year-old Mafu speaks through Penny Torres of Medford, Oregon. MariJo Donais, who lives in Vancouver, Washington, is the channel for forty-thousand-year-old Zanzoona.[11]

From its first stirrings in the late 1960s, the contemporary New Age movement has become widespread and increasingly intrusive in American culture. On New Year's Day in 1987, seven thousand people paid five dollars each to gather in the Seattle Kingdome at four o'clock in the morning to pray, meditate, and otherwise "visualize" peace into existence. J. Z. Knight took center stage as she channeled Ramtha on national television. Major bookstores now offer sections on New Age or metaphysics. Moving Books, a Seattle book distributor that specializes in New Age reading, sends out about two thousand titles each day to bookstores primarily in the United States and Canada.[12]

A desire for spiritual insight, knowledge about the future, and understanding to dispel their confusion lead people to look into these kinds of "messages" from past ages. According to the Bible, there are no beings called Ramtha, Mafu, and Zanzoona unless they are demons in disguise. The biblical explanation is that these beings are powerful demons that have control of people. The desire for spiritual "high energy" that is manifested in the New Age phenomenon has attracted people to believe that "everything is energy and energy is God. Ergo, humans are gods, too."[13]

The movement has spawned new interest in such arcane activities as fortune-telling, firewalking, mental telepathy, and past-life therapy. The New Age has left its mark on bookstores, radio stations, and movie theaters. It has touched politics, has added phrases to our vocabulary, and has affected the way we think about the environment and how we treat our bodies.[14]

The New Age religion at its heart is nothing more than sophisticated demonic activity. Ed Murphy writes,

> The New Age movement is a satanic movement of self-deification diametrically opposed to Christianity. The terrible danger arises from its deceptive packaging. It even has infiltrated the Christian Church, and we need to remind our-

selves of those words of 1 John 4:1, "Beloved, do not believe every spirit, but test the spirits to see whether they are from God; because many false prophets have gone out into the world."[15]

It would appear that most human beings have a hunger for a relationship with God, and Satan knows that. He will create all kinds of religious thinking and spiritual experiences in order to confuse people about the truth. The New Age movement and the current interest in the occult illustrate this. Paul informs Timothy, "The spirit clearly says that in later times some will abandon the faith and follow deceiving spirits and things taught by demons" (1 Tim. 4:1). There will be not only demonic deception but also false miracles in the last days. Again, Paul warns, "The coming of the lawless one will be in accordance with the work of Satan displayed in all kinds of counterfeit miracles, signs and wonders, and in every sort of evil that deceives those who are perishing" (2 Thess. 2:9–10). Satan and his demonic cohorts will do everything they can to keep people from the truth found in Jesus Christ. They will continue to distract and tempt the church of Jesus Christ from reaching those who do not know Him.

How Powerful Is Satan?

THERE IS NO QUESTION that Satan is highly intelligent, understands human behavior, knows much about our weaknesses, and has a strategy to persuade people to follow him. The Bible calls him "the prince of this world" (John 12:31; 14:30), and he attempts to influence the nations to do his will. His last-ditch attempt to control this world is described in Revelation 20:7–10. Satan will be permitted by God to try to deceive the nations to resist Christ's kingdom. But he will fail and will finally be cast into the "lake of burning sulfur" that is prepared for the devil and his angels.

Satan controls the principalities and powers of the air, and there is good reason to believe that he has an organizational plan to carry out his desires. The account in Daniel 10 about "the prince of Persia" and Michael the archangel, which we observed in the previous chapter, seems to indicate that Satan assigns his demons to different parts of the world. The Bible provides no details as to possible strategies or what types of demons are assigned to the various locations.

We do well not to try to figure out all the possible demonic activity in any given part of the world. Scripture provides only enough information for us to understand that Satan has a plan; we have no specifics. That is for the better because our focus must be on Jesus Christ, not on what the devil might be up to. The early church was consumed with Jesus and with reaching the people who did not know Him; they did not focus on the devil. (The names of Satan and the devil are used only four times in the book of Acts.) Those early Christians were surely aware of the devil's devices and knew that he could attack them at any given moment. But they were not trying to figure out how to "map" cities (locating the different demonic strongholds in various communities) or to find out the names of the demons involved in a particular place. Rather, they were concerned to bring an effective gospel witness to the lost.

The Spiritual Struggle for Cities

SOME CITIES IN THE world today are very dark with spiritual oppression. The gospel has not had much effect in those places, and consequently Satan has gained much control. In some of the cities I have visited, there was hardly any Christian witness and I felt the spiritual oppression. However, I have also been in cities where there was very little spiritual oppression because there were dynamic churches and great things happening for God. Neither Satan nor his demons could do much there.

We must realize that the church is the answer to running demonic forces out of a community. The church consists of born-again Christians who are living in the light. When the church is alive, the darkness over a community begins to go away. Satan and his demonic followers will attempt to hinder the Christian witness, but God is on the side of the church. In the same way that God intervened when Daniel's answer to prayer was being hindered, He will see Christians through when they are being opposed by the devil today.

David Yonggi Cho of Seoul, Korea, is pastor of the largest church in the history of the world. More than 700,000 people attend Yoido Full Gospel Church. Fifty years ago, Korea was one of the most spiritually bankrupt countries in the world. Now many estimate that more than half its population are born-again Christians. Dr. Cho and many others paid a tremendous price to influence that country for God. No one would have ever guessed that God would use this man in the way He has. Cho writes:

> In 1958, I went to a suburb of Seoul, Korea, to start a church. As soon as I put up a tent for our meetings, the kingdom of darkness challenged me.
>
> "You can't start a church here!" I was told by the priest of a heathen temple. "We have been here for many years. We have dominion over this area. If you build a church here, we will destroy it. We will hurt you. We can even kill you."
>
> But I was not afraid. I was praying very hard. We kept up our confrontation like two children fighting each other.
>
> Finally, the priest said, "Let's have a contest. You have been preaching that your God is the living God and that Jesus Christ is the same yesterday, today and forever. This is our proposition:
>
> "Down there in the town is a woman who has been paralyzed for many years. She gave birth to a small girl and both of them are now dying.
>
> "If you go there and raise her up and make her healthy within one month, we will give you permission to have your church here. Other-wise, you must leave. Are you ready to accept our challenge?"
>
> They were grinning. They knew they had trapped me. I had no place to escape.
>
> But I said, "OK, I'll accept your challenge. When I raise that woman in the name of Jesus Christ and she is healed, then you should leave this area."

Believing I could never raise her up, they accepted my counter-proposal.

We were now really engaged in spiritual warfare. Physically, you could see the priest of the heathen temple and his followers, but behind them was the kingdom of darkness. As for me, I was not alone. I was incorporated into the Kingdom of the Son of God, so the Kingdom of God was behind me.

Every day I was praying almost 21 hours. I did not go home. I stayed in the church with one blanket, and I slept there.

I began going to the home of this woman and her daughter. She was the most miserable human being I ever met. They never cleaned the house and the smell was just awful.

So we cleaned the home. We cooked a good meal, and I tried very nicely to preach Jesus Christ to her.

But she was adamant. "No, I will not accept Jesus Christ," she insisted. "I'd rather die in this situation."

When I left, the heathen priest came.

"Stand against the Christians," he would say. "Don't accept Christianity. Once you receive Jesus you and your family will be annihilated by our god."

We were really in a battle over her. I visited in the morning, and they visited in the afternoon. I prayed, and I preached about Jesus Christ, trying to sow some seeds of faith. Then this demon would come and take away all the seeds.

One week passed, two weeks passed and then three weeks. The 29th day came and still nothing had happened.

Oh, I became desperate. They were shouting the victory. They were smiling. They were ready to come and take away our tent church. Though our faith remained strong, our small group of Christians was at a loss as to what to do.

Early in the morning of the 30th day I was fighting and struggling in this spiritual warfare. "Father," I prayed, "If You will not perform a miracle, then the children of God will get all the shame before these people. So You've got to come and do something."

Then I fell into a trance. In my trance, I saw the door of my room open and a big, terrible snake came dancing into the room to the sound of some very eerie oriental music.

The head of the snake was a woman more beautiful than I had ever seen before. But the body was a snake. This woman was beautifully smiling at me and she said, "Let's live together. Let us not fight each other. I can accommodate you. We can compromise and have a very happy life."

But I said, "You are a snake and a human being. I can never live together with you."

Suddenly, the facial features were changed into a most ugly devil. The snake jumped up on me. I took it by the neck, but it was powerfully pushing itself towards me. I felt so paralyzed that I could not even speak.

The snake seemed ready to bite my head off, so inside my heart I cried, "Lord, save me! Jesus! Jesus!" At the Name of Jesus I saw fear appear in the eyes of the snake. I was given strength to mention the name of Jesus verbally. "Jesus, Jesus!"

The snake lost its power and slumped down on the floor. I put my heel on its head and smashed it. I rolled it up on my arm and took it out of the house where people had gathered from all over town.

"You have been worshipping this snake generation after generation," I said to them as I cast the snake down. "From today, the snake is defeated. You must now believe in Jesus Christ, the son of God."

When I awoke from the trance, I saw it was around 4:30 a.m. so I hurriedly got dressed and went to conduct our early morning prayer meeting. Dozens of people were there.

Just as we were completing the prayer time, a woman of our church rushed up and said, "Now, pastor, we are finished. They are all marching towards us to destroy the church."

I rushed out to see a crowd led by a slim woman carrying a child in her bosom. As they came nearer, I could hardly believe my eyes. This woman had the identical facial features as the one dying with paralysis. "They must be twins," I thought.

"Pastor, do you recognize me?" she said as she bowed before me.

"You look exactly like that woman who was dying from paralysis," I answered.

"I am that woman," she said.

"At two o'clock last evening you came to our yard. You shouted to me, 'Rise up in the name of Jesus Christ.' So I rose up. I saw I was completely healed. I took up my child and could push her above my head. She was also healed.

"I began crying and shouting. The power of the Lord came on me. I was shaking and had a warm sensation all over my body. I kicked the door open to meet you, but you were already gone."

I knew I had not gone there last night. I now realized that this was not my own battle, but a corporate battle with Jesus Christ, the Holy Spirit and the angels of God. They fought against the kingdom of darkness and won.

The woman went from house to house, giving testimony of what Jesus had done. The whole town turned out and followed her. What a revival we had!

By now the priests had fled. We marched to the heathen temple on the hill. The people burned it down and gave the property to me. Later, we built a memorial church that seated 5,000. The whole area turned to Christ and became our church members. The building still stands.[16]

There is no question that this experience of Pastor Cho was a battle with demons. Satan's demons had had control over that city perhaps for centuries, but a man came because he wanted to reach the lost with the gospel of Jesus Christ. Satan attempted to intimidate him and bring fear into his life, but he stood steadfast in prayer. As a result, countless people have been reached and set free from demonic deception and control.

We, too, may be attacked by demons. Paul tells us that we are in a combat "against the spiritual forces of evil in the heavenly realms" (Eph. 6:12). However, in our personal spiritual battles, we can know that we are not alone. As Christians we have the Holy Spirit that dwells within us, and He will help us every day if we turn to Him. The demons' sophisticated twenty-first-century activity is no match for the eternal Holy Spirit's power.

FOUR ⊹

Satan's Plan
of Attack

For two years my friend, whom I'll call Allan, had felt exhausted. He was the pastor of a large church that had quickly grown to several thousand people. He had spearheaded a major building program, and because he wanted to be sure everything was done right, he worked directly with the contractors. When that was added to all his other responsibilities as the pastor of a thriving church, he became "burned out."

Allan became discouraged, lost sleep, and felt that he was on an emotional downward spiral. Even though the church was growing and the building was going up, he battled with his confidence and sense of security. He was praying and reading his Bible, but couldn't get over the despondency. He was exhausted.

Instead of confiding in lifelong friends who would have dropped almost anything to get him some help, Allan withdrew into himself and hid from them. His thoughts were, "I can get through this. I've been down before and have pulled through. After the building program is completed, everything will settle down again."

Adding to the pressure was the fact that his next of kin was dying, and Allan became this relative's guardian and supervisor. This relative was not a Christian.

The hectic schedule opened the door for the enemy to attack my friend. To add to his physical and emotional struggle, a hurting woman disclosed her affection for him. Allan found himself battling conflicting emotions. Even though the incident was minor and brief, he felt confused in his thinking and immediately became convicted about his behavior. He walked away from what could have been an even greater tragedy. He confessed his thoughts to his wife and soon confessed to the church. He soon resigned from his pastorate and sought help to overcome his burnout and to build strengths that would prevent this from happening again. He left his career in the ministry, sought the help he needed, and today is doing well with his family still together.[1]

This story is certainly not unique. Countless people around the world have had similar experiences. What this middle-aged pastor did not realize is that the enemy of his soul was looking for a way to destroy him. Satan took advantage of my friend's weariness, discouragement, and vulnerability to tempt him in a way that he had never been tempted. The devil knew that if he could persuade Allan to become involved with another woman, not only would the pastor become deceived and possibly ruined, but a "Christian leader" would fall. A prominent family would become devastated, a church would become disillusioned, and the Christian testimony that a church had worked decades to build would be greatly injured.

Satan takes his time to watch and wait for the opportunity to tempt or attack. He has no concern about a person's weakened state of mind. He only wants to come in for the kill.

Someone has said, "I don't mind going to war, I just want to know who my enemy is!" Understanding the enemy's primary ways of attacking is key to winning the battle. In Ephesians 6:13 Paul tells Christians to put on the whole armor of God so that when that day of evil comes (and it will come to each of us), we will be able to stand our ground. In other words, we can anticipate Satan's attack and consequently we need to be on constant alert, knowing it could come at any time. However, if we do not believe there is a devil or that he is specifically interested in us, then, like a sniper in war, he can target us and pick us off one at a time.

Fifty-five percent of Americans believe in the existence of Satan, and 82 percent profess to believe in an afterlife that includes both heaven and hell. Forty-six percent believe they will spend eternity in heaven, and only 4 percent believe they will go to hell for eternity. Hell is not something very many Americans honestly fear,[2] and few people realize that Satan has a personal agenda for them.

Satan's Goal for Nonbelievers

THE DEVIL'S PRIMARY GOAL is to keep non-Christians blind to a saving faith in Christ[3] and to keep Christians from all that God intends them to be. The Scripture makes it clear that the enemy of our souls has been defeated by Christ's victory over sin and death on the cross (1 John 3:8; Heb. 2:14–15). Yet, Satan is fiercer than ever before and has intensified his strategy because he knows his end is near; he understands that his time to work is short. Oswald Chambers said, "It is never wise to underestimate an enemy. We look upon the enemy of our souls as a conquered foe; so he is, but only to God, not to us."[4]

This spiritual enemy will do everything in his power to distract, deceive, and destroy those who do not know Christ. He knows that if they become Christians, they will not only be delivered from his clutches but become a threat to him. If Satan needs to bring a temporary pleasure or secret sin into their lives in order to control or deceive them, he will arrange it. Deception is his specialty. Deceit is his character.

My father[5] understood the shallow friendships that heavy drinking can bring, and he experienced firsthand the emptiness of alcohol addiction. Night after night, as the manager of two bars, he opened the Ransford Cocktail Lounge and the Dutch Room in Brainerd, Minnesota.

As a boy Dad attended a German Lutheran Sunday school. He married a staunch Catholic. They had my brother, Ray, first and then me. But because of complications during my birth, my mother was dying. As many people do when they come face to face with death, she prayed, "God, if you will let me live to raise Tom, I will serve you."

God heard my mother's prayer and spared her life. A few years later, my parents rented an apartment from a Christian woman.

This landlady had a "no smoking" rule, but my parents—both chain smokers—lied to her and therefore were granted a lease. Often Mom and Dad would sit by the screen window and blow the cigarette smoke out through the window. They knew that if they were caught, they would be kicked out.

One day the landlady invited my mother to a revival meeting at the church she attended. Mother consented to going, and although it was very different from her religious background, she liked what she heard and how she felt. She was invited back a second night, and when the invitation to accept Jesus Christ was given, she went to the front of the church in response. As Mother was kneeling at the altar of that church, she didn't know how to pray—all she knew was the rosary.

Mother began to pray the rosary and someone said, "Beatrice, you don't need to pray the rosary, you can talk to Jesus directly." She was amazed that God could do that for her, and she gave her life to Christ. She knew her life would never be the same. Later that evening, when Dad came home from the bar, Mother told him what had happened to her. He threw a fit: "If you have gotten religion, I don't want any part of this marriage! I'm packing my bags and leaving!"

Dad went into the other room and began packing. My parents didn't have many possessions, and I believe there was only five dollars in the house. My mother followed Dad to the front door, pleading, "Waldo, please stay! The boys need a father. Don't leave me. Please stay for the sake of the boys."

Dad stood there in silence and decided to stay—for a while. The next day, when Mother explained that she felt the Lord had helped her quit smoking, Dad blew cigarette smoke in her face. He was pretty upset.

When Dad went to work at the bar, Mother and the landlady prayed for him. "Lord, please save Waldo, and help him know how much you love him." Mother explained, "He thinks that I have just 'got religion.' He doesn't understand that I have found a personal relationship with Christ." The landlady comforted my mother and encouraged her to keep praying.

Early Sunday morning, Dad came home from the bar and couldn't sleep. He tossed and turned in bed, feeling terribly convicted about his life. Finally he got up and knelt beside the bed. He knew he wanted to pray but didn't know how. All he could remember was the Lord's Prayer that he had learned in Sunday school more than twenty years earlier. He hadn't been in church since then. Dad prayed, "Our Father, who art in heaven, hallowed is your name. Thy kingdom come, Thy will be done, on earth as it is in heaven. Give us this day our daily bread, and forgive us our debts as we forgive our debtors. And do not lead us into temptation, but deliver us from the evil one, for Thine is the Kingdom and the power, and the glory, forever!" When dad prayed that prayer, which had been hidden in the back of his memory, he gave his life to Christ as well.

Dad had a miraculous experience and was immediately delivered from alcoholism and chain smoking. He told Mother about his decision to serve Jesus, and you can imagine her joy and excitement that God had answered her prayers. Dad and Mother began a new life together, this time walking the Christian walk. They became very involved in the local church, and Dad eventually became a deacon. Not long after, they felt they should enter the full-time ministry.

Recently Dad received a fiftieth anniversary pin for ministry in the Assemblies of God. Over the years Dad and Mother pioneered several churches in Minnesota. As an evangelist he held revival meetings in 117 of the 138 churches in that state. Thousands of people have made decisions to follow Christ because of my parents' ministry.

Dad and Mom changed their parenting techniques, too, and instilled in all their children a desire to serve God. My brother Ray and I have both been in full-time ministry for many years. My sister and her husband are pastors. Several of the grandchildren are in ministry as well. The story of what happened to this barroom alcoholic and his young Catholic wife has touched a multitude of people. Their decision to serve Christ and to stay together began a ripple effect that will go on and on for generations. This is why

Satan will do anything he can to keep those without Christ spiritually blind. The enemy knows God's potential in a person's life and will distract people from the truth whenever possible.

Satan's Goal for Believers

FOR CHRISTIANS, SATAN'S BATTLE strategy changes somewhat. This enemy is aware that he has lost ground with believers because of the power of Christ in their lives. Paul writes, "For he has rescued us from the dominion of darkness and brought us into the kingdom of the Son he loves" (Col. 1:13). Moreover, "in Christ all the fullness of the Deity lives in bodily form, and you have been given fullness in Christ, who is the head over every power and authority" (Col. 2:9–10).

Because Satan cannot force Christians back into his domain, he tries to keep believers from reaching their full potential in Christ. Paul admonished the Corinthian believers that they should be careful to forgive one another, "in order that Satan might not outwit us. For we are not unaware of his schemes" (2 Cor. 2:11). Satan can outsmart us if we are not aware of his deceptive tactics.

We do ourselves a disservice when we think that the enemy attacks the saints as a group and doesn't pay much attention to individuals. Satan hates us. He will accuse and tempt us where and when he believes we are most vulnerable. He enjoys challenging us one on one when we are alone and not part of the crowd. Paul said that *our struggle* is not against flesh and blood, but against the rulers, against the authorities, against the powers of this dark world" (Eph 6:12, italics added). "Our struggle" is an individual battle. In the sport of wrestling, the wrestler is part of a team, but he must do battle individually. He trains with a team and has a team coach, but when he goes out on that mat, he is alone with his opponent. Wrestling is close combat, and similarly every believer throughout life must be involved in close combat with the enemy of their souls. The enemy will try every move he can to get us flat on our backs, but we can win the match. As believers we belong to Christ, and God will be our helper, our rearguard. If the enemy tries any trick moves behind our backs, God will take care of him.

Throughout Scripture we see godly people who understood that they should not try to manage their lives without God's blessing and approval. Even though Moses was given many promises about the next step he was to take in his life, he said, "If your Presence does not go with us, do not send us up from here" (Exod. 33:15). David knew that he was God's appointed king but he still sought God's help with a person who was trying to undermine him: "O LORD, turn Ahithophel's counsel into foolishness" (2 Sam. 15:31). By contrast, Saul lost his kingdom because he did not follow God's rules for leading. He thought he could be successful without the Lord's help (1 Sam. 15) and did not follow the instructions God had given him. Just as Saul was wrong, so are we if we believe we can win in a match against the enemy without the help of God. To win in our struggles we must use all the help God offers. We can only be victorious because, in Paul's words, "I can do everything through him who gives me strength" (Phil. 4:13).

The Three Main Ways Satan Attacks People

Satan opposes. THE NAME *Satan* means opposer. The moment that Lucifer decided to oppose the ways of God was the day of his fall. Satan will attempt to oppose God's truth, God's ways, and God's kingdom on earth. The Christian must understand that this opposer is their chief opponent. George Sweeting writes,

> Satan opposes God's authority, His word, His work, His people, His glory and His will. Satan has always opposed the plan of God. He tempted the Lord Jesus in the wilderness (Mt. 4), and his temptations were designed to thwart God's plan of redemption. He takes away the Word of God from the hearts of those who hear it (Mt. 13:19); and he sows seeds of falsehood (v. 3–8).[6]

It is Satan who blinds the minds of unbelievers so they cannot see the truth in Jesus Christ (2 Cor. 4:4). Missionaries around the world understand his attempts to disrupt their plans for God. Satan opposes the church by sowing disunity among believers. He encourages unforgiveness, bitterness, envy, strife, deceit, and hatred in God's people in order to oppose God's righteous ways. Satan is also a master at challenging the Christian who wants to live a Christ-honoring life or wants to be a witness to a friend or relative.

Through his own audacity to oppose his Creator God and through thousands of years of practice, Satan has devised both common and unusual ways to be against anything that God is for.

Satan accuses. In the oldest book in the Bible we read the amazing story of Satan's personal attack on Job's life. Scripture says that Job "was blameless and upright; he feared God and shunned evil" (Job 1:1). However, Satan accused him to God by saying that he was only serving God because of all the blessings in his life. Satan might have said something like this to God: "Job has false motives for serving You. He is just doing it because You have given him so much and You protect him. Take it away, and he will walk away from you."

God knew Job's motives because He knows the heart of everyone. As for Job's commitment to Him, God said to Satan, "There is no one on earth like him" (v. 8). God knew Job would always serve and be faithful to Him, so He gave Satan permission to take away Job's earthly possessions. Satan viciously attacked Job and destroyed his health, his children, and most of his possessions. Job surprised Satan by not breaking under this kind of loss and oppression. The Bible says, "He still maintains his integrity.... In all this, Job did not sin in what he said" (Job 2:3, 10).

God was right about Job. Satan the accuser was wrong, but he thought it was worth a try. After this incredible attack from Satan, God made Job "prosperous again and gave him twice as much as he had before.... The LORD blessed the latter part of Job's life more than the first" (Job 42:10, 12).

The devil has not changed over the centuries. Satan is called the "accuser of our brothers, who accuses them before our God" (Rev. 12:10). He charges believers with offense, error, wrongdoing, failure, sin, and wrong motives. He cannot comprehend God's complete forgiveness and willingness to justify those who turn to Christ. Yet the Bible states that Christians are "without blemish and free from accusation" (Col. 1:22).

It's almost as if Satan is saying to God, "That's not fair—they have sinned! You know they have sinned. You have to judge them! They deserve what I'll give them." Actually, Satan is partially right in his accusations against us. Our evil behavior and greedy motives keep us from fellowship with God. Paul says that the wicked— those belonging to Satan's kingdom—will not inherit the kingdom of God. "Do not be deceived: Neither the sexually immoral nor idolaters nor adulterers nor male prostitutes nor homosexual offenders nor thieves nor the greedy nor drunkards nor slander- ers nor swindlers will inherit the kingdom of God" (1 Cor. 6:9– 10). However, the wonderful truth is that, with God's help, people can be forgiven and can change from their sinful behavior. Paul reveals an amazing fact about those who were bound by sin: "And *that is what some of you were.* But you were washed, you were sanctified, you were justified in the name of the Lord Jesus Christ and by the Spirit of our God" (v. 11, italics added).

In the case of my dad, the devil can say—and has said—to him, "You have been a drunk, you have cursed, and you almost walked out on your family." My father responds to these attempts to discourage him by saying, "Yes, I did those things, but Jesus has broken the power of sin in my life, He has forgiven me, and I am His child now, not yours!"

Satan will accuse the adulterer, saying what he or she has done is unforgivable. He will tell the former homosexual who has come to Christ that he cannot overcome this behavior. He will tell those who have habitually lied that this habit will follow them all their lives, and he will remind them that all liars go to hell. He will tell Christians who have fallen back into sin that they cannot be for- given again. He will take advantage of our weaknesses, mistakes, and sinful decisions. When this happens, we only need to look to Jesus Christ, who is our "advocate with the Father" (1 John 2:1 KJV); He will come to our defense when we seek His assistance with repentance and sincere hearts.

Satan can point his finger of accusation at us, but the fact remains that we who are in Christ are without blemish and free from accusation.

Satan imitates. Satan fell because he thought he could become as powerful as God and be like God. Since that original thought, Satan has tried to imitate God. He has his counterfeit miracles, signs, and wonders. He enabled Pharaoh's magicians to imitate the miracles that Moses performed through the power of God (Exod. 7:10–12). He will perform counterfeit miracles, signs, and wonders through the Antichrist (2 Thess. 2:9; Rev. 13:11–17). He does all this to deceive all he can so that they will give allegiance to him. Satan has invented literally thousands of religions and false gods in order to distract people from the truth. He has his own counterfeit ministers and church and gospel.

The devil also counterfeits many of God's principles and distorts them to fit his perverse agenda. Paul wrote to the Galatian church, "I am astonished that you are so quickly deserting the one who called you by the grace of Christ and are turning to a different gospel" (Gal. 1:6). Some people in that church had bought into a gospel promoted by Satan to distract them from the truth. Dr. Ron Carlson of Christian Ministries International, who has researched the subject of cults thoroughly, has found that many people who get caught up in cults have come from mainline Christian denominations but were not well grounded in the teachings of the Bible.[7] It appears that the devil understands that all human beings have an emptiness in their hearts until they come into a relationship with God.

There is a spiritual hunger in people's lives around the world. Understanding this truth, the enemy has developed thousands of counterfeit spiritual experiences and beliefs because he knows that many will think they have discovered the right way.

In a sick sense, this imitator thinks he can become "as God." He is a counterfeit and attempts to do the types of miracles God does. He endeavors to organize his kingdom in ways that have some resemblance with the ways God does things—that is, Satan has his own religions, teachings, gods (idols), ministers, prophets, and supernatural wonders. Satan's motives are evil, and he will destroy those who put their allegiance in him. He is a thief, and he invades people's lives "to steal, and kill, and destroy." By contrast, when Jesus comes into lives, He gives abundant life (John 10:10).

Satan is called a roaring lion, but Jesus is the lion of the tribe of Judah.

Lucifer was the son of the morning, but Jesus is the bright and morning Star.

Satan will have a city called Babylon the great, but Jesus has The New Jerusalem.

The Angel of Light

THIS IMITATOR WHO COMES as an angel of light can be very difficult to recognize. He will take advantage of people's grief, sorrow, naïveté, and ignorance in order to trick them.

A woman we will call Carol made an appointment with me a few months after her husband of thirty years passed away. I anticipated that she would still be grieving and would need some comfort and encouragement. I thought that perhaps I could introduce her to some of her peers in the church. But as she entered my office, I sensed that she needed to talk to me about more than her grief. She wanted an explanation of something she had experienced.

"Pastor, I have just had the most wonderful thing happen to me!" Carol began.

Feeling somewhat excited for her, I said, "Tell me about it."

"I have spoken to my husband," she said with some hesitation. "I missed him so much, and there were many things that we did not have the opportunity to discuss before he died."

"Go on, Carol," I said. "What do you mean?"

She said, "I couldn't find things around the house—you know, things that only husbands know where they are. I even sensed that he was there, just like before, only I couldn't see him. At times I would talk to him ... but I heard nothing back. 'Henry,' I would say, 'where are the keys to that old car? I need to sell it.'"[8]

"So, how is it that you have talked to Henry?" I asked.

Carol responded hesitantly, with her eyes looking toward the floor. "I heard of this person that could contact Henry. My friend told me that she knew a person that could actually bring Henry back—you know, only his spirit—but I could have a conversation with him and tell him all the things I have been wanting to tell him and ask him some questions."

Carol was trying to gauge my reaction.

I said, "Go on, tell me what happened."

"Well, I thought about it and decided to do it. I know this seems weird, and you have even taught that we should not get involved with this sort of thing and that it is dangerous, but I really saw no harm."

"Carol, what did you experience?" I asked.

"Well, I met the person, and they did some kind of religious thing and said that they would be able to channel Henry's spirit to speak to me. I really didn't pay much attention to what was going on until something unbelievable happened. I asked specific questions that only Henry would know the answers to. The answers that came back were right!"

With tears in her eyes and a degree of satisfaction on her face, Carol was looking for my approval.

"Pastor, this must have been Henry. No one else could have known the answer to the questions I asked."

I said, "Carol, you loved Henry and had a tremendous marriage and lots of wonderful memories. He was a good man, and I know that you miss him terribly. I know that you feel there were things left unfinished when he died, and that is often the case. Death can come when it's not expected, and the grief that a loved one experiences cannot be really comprehended by anyone until they go through it."

I paused, not wanting her to misunderstand what I was about to say.

She said, "I know, Henry's death was so sudden. I wasn't ready because we had so much more to do."

I said, "Carol, I can appreciate how much you miss Henry, and how badly you want to speak to him, just one more time. But your experience was not a genuine experience. It was a deception provided by the enemy."

"But all the right answers were given!" Carol exclaimed.

"Carol," I said, "the devil took advantage of your grief and sorrow. You see, there are demons that live in an unseen world that can provide the answers to the kinds of questions you were asking. They will do this in order to convince you that we can talk to our departed loved ones. The person that you talked to, the channeler, was nothing more than a witch who had a demonically inspired gift to let a demon speak through her."

Carol didn't want to believe me, but continued to listen.

"You see, demons have been around for thousands of years. They are led by Satan. One of their primary goals is to deceive people. They even have the ability to appear to be something good, when their motives are terribly evil.

"Carol, the devil deceived you. You did not really talk to Henry. He is in heaven. You talked to a demon who ultimately wants your soul, and he will do anything in his power to trick you into leaving your experience with Christ."

I gently went on. "You must rebuke this experience, promise that you will never do this again, and ask God's forgiveness. I will pray for you, too, that this experience will not have any more effect on your life and that God will protect you from the enemy's attack."

I was grateful that Carol believed me. She understood what I said to her and promised never to take part in this kind of activity again.[9]

Carol had had an experience with the great imitator, the deceiver who takes advantage of people's weaknesses.

Satan would like people to believe that *every* miracle is from God, yet he has the power to perform counterfeit signs and wonders. This fact should cause us to be careful to evaluate every supernatural occurrence to see whether it is of God or Satan. John tells us to "test the spirits to see whether they are from God, because many false prophets have gone out into the world" (1 John 4:1).

Discerning the Spirits

THERE IS A CHARISMA gift that God gives to people in the body of Christ called the gift of discernment—"the ability to distinguish between spirits" (1 Cor. 12:10). Christians are able to discern and test with the Word of God whether an experience is from God or from the enemy. We can avoid being deceived by Satan's lies and counterfeit miracles if we know the Word of God well and examine all that we hear, see, and sense on the basis of Scripture. We can know that we are in safe territory. God gave us His inspired Word, and it "is useful for teaching, rebuking, correcting and training in righteousness, so that the man of God may be thoroughly equipped for every good work" (2 Tim. 3:16–17).

George Sweeting said, "Satan specializes in religion—false religion. He is subtle. And it is just that subtlety that makes him so deadly. Although most people think of the devil as something ugly and horribly evil, he is not always like that. He is not a little red man with a trident and a tail."[10]

The Antichrist

THE PERSON WHO WILL literally amaze the world in the last days will be a man John the apostle calls "the antichrist" (1 John 2:18, 22).

Donald Stamps writes about the Antichrist, "It is possible these demonstrations of the supernatural will be seen on television around the world. Millions will be impressed, deceived, and persuaded by this highly persuasive and popular leader because they have no deep commitment to or love for the truth of God's Word."[11] The Antichrist will be controlled by Satan and will in turn oppose anything that is truly Christian. He will be an accuser and an imitator. He will even enter into the temple (which will be newly built during his lifetime) in Jerusalem and enter the holy place and declare himself to be God (2 Thess. 2:4). This devil-possessed human being will attempt to imitate God. Satan will use this person to administer his end-time strategy.

Satan's primary tactics of opposition, accusation, and imitation are meant to keep people from Christ and to discourage Christians so as to become impotent in their faith. God wants us to be aware of Satan's battle strategy and to be confident in His incredible power to destroy the enemy's attempts to deceive and discourage us. During the time that the Antichrist rules this world, he will do everything in his power to destroy the true believers in Christ. A multitude of people will turn to Jesus Christ after the "rapture" of the church because they will realize that the Christians were right. They will remember how a Christian friend told them about Jesus and taught that there would be an event called the rapture. With this memory, many will give their lives to Christ. They will go through persecution such as this world has never known.

The Antichrist's system will be set up to kill believers in Christ. Even though masses of believers will die, they will win this battle against the enemy. John writes, "They overcame him by the blood of the Lamb and by the word of their testimony; they did not love their lives so much as to shrink from death" (Rev. 12:11).

You might think, "But I have so many problems of my own. It seems that Satan has attacked me in every one of these ways. How can I stand a chance against such a powerful being?" Be assured that you not only stand a chance, but can win—with God's help. Many people have suffered every bit as much as you. The Lord has shown them the way to become overcomers. In the remaining chapters of this book we discover the keys to living a victorious life.

FIVE ✦

Assaulting the Church

For years Pastor Tommy Barnett had felt a concern for the city of Los Angeles. He is the pastor of a church of more than ten thousand members in Phoenix, Arizona, and knew it was impossible for him to pastor a church in both cities at the same time. His twenty-two-year-old son, Matthew, felt a similar concern for the needs of L.A. Both father and son felt that the gang killings, the drug trafficking, the prostitution, and the devastation of many people who lived in this city had to be curtailed. They knew Los Angeles was a prime location for a unique, dynamic church.

When Tommy was visiting a wise pastor in that city, he was cautioned that Los Angeles was the devil's jewel and pride. The pastor told him, "If you come here, you will have the greatest fight of your life." Tommy took note of what his friend had said but decided to look for a way to begin the church.

Matthew moved to the inner city of L.A., and Tommy continued to pastor the church in Phoenix while flying into Los Angeles to help Matt every Thursday through Saturday. Their schedules were exhausting, but the results made their efforts seem worthwhile. Within months, hundreds of people were attending services. Prostitutes, street people, bikers, the poor, and the wealthy—all were coming to know Christ. In just a few months, more than a hundred other ministries from the Los Angeles area had decided to work together to help the city.

This coalition needed a building and heard of an old hospital that was for sale. The hospital was huge—more than 70 percent of the babies born in L.A. before 1980 had been born there. It was being used occasionally as a set for movies or television. The purchase price was several million dollars, but the building would fit the coalition's dream of making a place of refuge for the hungry, homeless, and the desperate. It would be a center of ministry, where a variety of Christian ministries could come together with one purpose. It would enable many ethnic congregations and language groups to worship in the same building but in different chapels.

With the help of many friends throughout the country, the coalition was able to buy the hospital. Today thousands make that facility their church home, and the "Dream Center" is having a major impact on East Los Angeles.

After one Sunday service, Matthew was approached by a man he had never seen. The man said to him, "I am going to make you very popular in this city and throughout the nation."

Matthew asked the man to explain what he meant. The man pulled a handgun from under his coat and showed it to Matthew. He said, "I'm dying of AIDS, and after one of your services I'm going to walk up to the front of the church and stand on the platform and kill myself. When the city hears about that, it will bring the church a lot of attention."

Matthew tried to counsel the man, who was obviously confused and overwhelmed with his condition. "Sir, please do not do that—we can help you. We will do anything we can to get you what you need."

The dying man then pointed the gun at Matthew and said, "I have a better idea, I will walk up to you and shoot you first and then me. That will really bring attention to this place."

Matthew was shocked, but he could tell by the look on the man's face and how he pointed the gun that he was serious. Matthew said quietly, "Well, sir, you can do that, but I know where I am going. I'm going to heaven when I die. Do you know where you are going?"

Matthew looked into the man's eyes and paused for a moment, then added, "I'm not afraid of you. I want to help you."

This made the man angry. He turned and hurried from the room, calling out over his shoulder, "I'll be back soon and I'm going to *do it!*"

Matthew didn't know what to think. He was shaking inside and told some of the leaders what had happened. They prayed about the situation and committed it to God. The thoughts still haunted Matthew. He wondered if the man would come back, and he had to fight being distracted because any service could be the chosen one when the man would try it. How would Matthew know? The congregation was large, and people are difficult to recognize in a crowd. All of this worried Matthew, but he was able to commit the matter to God in prayer.

Within a few weeks the man did come back. But this time his reason was different. He had felt so convicted about what he had done to Matthew that he talked to one of the leaders and gave his life to Christ. The man then went to a care facility in another city where people were suffering from devastating illnesses such as AIDS. This man is no longer confused, nor does he want to take his life—or Matthew's. He is looking forward to going to the heaven Matthew told him about.

Satan would have loved to encourage that man to carry out his former plan. Satan was behind the man's confusion and the lies he believed. The Dream Center is invading Satan's territory, and he doesn't like it. Satan's darkness is dispelled, and God's light is shining brighter in Los Angeles.[1]

Tommy Barnett reminded us that the pastor's warning came true. "This has been the greatest battle of my life. I have never experienced such spiritual warfare, such weariness, and so much personal attack from the enemy. But it's worth it! Look at the changed lives!"

Satan hates the church because he hates Jesus Christ. The body of Christ on earth is made up of men and women who are born again. They are diverse; there is no denominational tag. The church is not a building; it is people who love Jesus Christ and have made Him their Lord. Satan wants to shame the church and destroy the effects of this mighty force in this world. He carefully looks for ways to ruin an individual believer or a group of believers who worship together. The church is the only entity left in the world that brings an awareness of the darkness that Satan represents. The church constantly marches into spiritually dark areas of the world and has a godly influence, not only on individual lives, but on communities as well.

Recently I preached in a church that is seeing thousands of people come to Christ. Along with the tremendous growth in that church and other churches in the community, it is reported that the crime rate has dropped about 20 percent there. Satan is very aware that good Christians make good citizens. A revival in a church is the greatest threat to his work in a community.

The Persecuted Church

IN MANY PLACES IN the world, the growing Christian church is being persecuted and thousands of Christians are being murdered. We might not think that the twenty-first-century church would go through this kind of barbaric experience, but the statistics tell a different story. The World Evangelical Fellowship recently stated that "the twentieth-century church faces increased persecution and that more Christians have been martyred for their faith in this century than in the previous 1900 years combined."[2]

"Christians are in fact the most persecuted religious group in the world today, with the greatest number of victims," asserts Nina Shea, director of the Puebla Program on Religious Freedom operated by Freedom House.[3]

Kim Lawson of *Christianity Today* writes, "Increasingly, Christians are harassed, arrested, interrogated, imprisoned, fined, or killed because of their religious beliefs and practices."[4]

Christianity is spreading in Indonesia, and the church has grown to include almost 12 percent of the population in the last five years.[5] However, along with this phenomenal growth there is increased persecution. In one incident it was reported that a mob of Muslims destroyed 10 church buildings and crippled a pastor in Indonesia. The 1000-strong mob attacked during Sunday services, tearing apart church buildings and setting fire to nearby cars and other vehicles. Government officials said that churches that do not have police protection should suspend meetings, but it is unclear whether police protection will be given. Government and Muslim leaders have been working to counter the rapid spread of Christianity in the country.[6]

In a majority of Persian Gulf countries, converting to Christianity is a crime. Under Islamic regulations an apostate who refuses to repent and return to Islam must be forcibly divorced from his wife, lose all his family inheritance rights, and relinquish custody of his Muslim children. It is reported that "an Islamic court in Kuwait proclaimed Hussein Qambar Ali, 44, an official apostate from Islam, because of his conversion to Christianity."

Apostasy is not illegal under the Kuwaiti constitution, but Muslims there nevertheless consider it an offense punishable by death. Islamic law would not hold anyone libel for killing an apostate—someone who has abandoned Islam for another faith.[7] Therfore Hussein has remained in hiding for several months.

Shortly before he died, Haik Hovsepian Mehr, the general superintendent of the Assemblies of God in Iran, spoke of the reason for church growth in that country. He wrote,

> Matthew 16:18 has proved to be wonderfully true for the Iranian church, "I will build my church; and the gates of hell shall not prevail against it." Muslim fundamentalists have tried to put pressure on the church of Jesus Christ, but they have not prevailed in their attempts to destroy it.
>
> Their first strategy was to expel all missionaries. . . . A second tactic was to close the Iranian Bible Society and all Christian bookstores. They then interrogated and intimated pastors and church leaders. Evangelism efforts were forbidden, except in church buildings. . . . They told church leaders that Muslims could not attend their services or inquire about the Christian faith. . . . All church leaders were pressured by

the authorities to write letters of appreciation for their religious freedom in Iran.[8]

Missionary Mark Bliss interviewed Haik about the persecution in Iran.

Mark: Do you think Satan has purposed to destroy the church in Iran, especially in the last few years?

Haik: Clearly the enemies of the cross are trying to find ways to close all churches that will not bow to them. Satan has always tried to destroy the saints in Iran [present-day Persia]. Daniel in the lion's den, Esther and Mordecai's experience with Haman, and the threats of Nehemiah's enemies are three Old Testament examples of attacks on God's people in Iran. But in all three instances the devil was defeated. I believe history is being repeated, and we will see great marvels in these last days.

Mark: What do you think is the reason for God's blessing on His church in Iran and its continued growth?

Haik: The main reason is that God promised to build His church in Iran, and I know He will do so. But a second reason is related to the suffering for Christ with joy which God is permitting us to experience. Revelation 12:11 mentions these three steps in our victory over the devil: "the blood of the Lamb," "the word of their [believers'] testimony," and their refusal to "love their lives so much as to shrink from death." When a Christian reaches a point where he can sacrifice himself for the Lord, then claiming power in the blood and giving a bold, clear testimony will easily follow.

Mark: Do you see any outstanding demonstrations of courageous Christian conviction?

Haik: Many members of the church, especially Muslim converts, are strong in their resistance. After Pastor Hossein Soodmand was hanged for his faith in December 1990, a believer approached me with tears in his eyes. "I wanted to be the first martyr, but Soodmand is the first now," he said. This same man was imprisoned for 45 days. His crime was selling 200 New Testaments.[9]

On January 19, 1994, Haik left his home to meet a guest at the airport in Teheran. He never returned. On Sunday, January 30, the

Teheran Office of Investigation notified Haik's family that he had died ten days earlier. Photographs used to identify Haik showed stitches along the abdomen. The marks were explained this way: "These could be the marks of an autopsy, torture, or both."

Authorities will only say that Haik died on January 20, with no explanation as to why the family was not notified until ten days later. "The questions surrounding Haik's disappearance and death may be mysterious, but they point strongly to the work of the government security forces," one source said.

The Iranian government had several motives to silence Haik. He had recently become more vocal in demanding religious freedom in Iran. "We have nothing else to lose," he wrote in a letter. "We have been tolerant and kept silent, but nothing has changed. Please don't worry about me. I am quite ready for anything."

Haik led an effort to secure the release of Mehdi Dibaj, an Iranian national minister accused of insulting Islam, acting as a spy for the West, and apostasy. After ten years in jail in Sari, Iran (including two years of solitary confinement in an unlit cell), Dibaj was sentenced to be executed, according to a statement by the court on December 21, 1993.

At Haik's urging, governments and human rights organizations around the world were informed of the situation. Several governments, including the U.S. State Department, wrote letters to the Iranian government requesting Dibaj's release.

In response to the international pressure, Dibaj was released from prison on Sunday, January 16, 1994. He arrived at Haik's home in Teheran within two days. When Dibaj entered Haik's home in Teheran, fifty believers excitedly greeted him with a chorus,

> In the name of Jesus,
> In the name of Jesus,
> We have the victory!
> In the name of Jesus, in the name of Jesus, demons will have
>   to flee.
> If we stand on the name of Jesus, tell me who can stand
>   before us.

In the precious name of Jesus
We have the victory.

The following day Haik disappeared.

A reliable source said, "The Iranian government was furious over an invitation Haik had issued to the United Nations to send a special envoy to investigate the abuse of Christians and other minorities in Iran."

Before his death, Haik had said, "If we die or go to jail for our faith, we want the whole Christian world to know what is happening to their brothers and sisters in a country claiming to have religious freedom."

Haik added, "I will go quietly."

Our source said, "Mehdi Dibaj may have said it best while awaiting execution, 'It is a terrible waste for a Christian to die a natural death.'"[10]

Satan would like nothing better than to destroy the church. He has demonstrated this through the centuries by promoting persecution and the martyrdom of Christians.[11]

The Poison of False Teaching

IN SEEKING TO WEAKEN and destroy the church, Satan tries to deceive individual believers. Historically he has done this largely through false doctrine spread by false teachers, false apostles, and false prophets. These people are "wolves in sheep's clothing."

Writing to the Ephesian church, Paul warns that after he leaves, "savage wolves will come in among you and will not spare the flock. Even from your own number men will arise and distort the truth in order to draw away disciples after them. So be on your guard!" (Acts 20:29–31). If we have been in a church environment for very long, we have probably seen some of these people in action. They will do anything to draw a crowd in order to promote their teaching. They are interested in drawing attention to what they are doing, not to what Jesus can do and is doing. Often their pride and arrogance are obvious. At other times they use a pious false humility to appear holy.

One prominent false teacher was Joseph Smith, the founder of the Mormon faith. Smith claimed to have met an angel called Moroni. Moroni supposedly told him things that are different from what Scripture teaches and, in fact, contradict many parts of the Bible. Out of that "new" revelation came the *Book of Mormon*. Mormons believe that this book is divinely inspired and regard it as holy scripture. If an angel did indeed visit Smith, it was not an angel of God, but a demon.

According to Muslim tradition, Muhammad had a similar experience in that a so-called angel, named Gabriel, spoke with him. The Koran actually contains four different and sometimes contradictory accounts of what happened.[12] The angel supposedly told Muhammad to start a new religion called Islam that would be exalted above all other religions, including Christianity and Judaism. Cult experts Ed Decker and Ron Carlson write,

> Muslims say, Muhammad received revelations during which he would go into epileptic fits. (That is what Muslims believe they were). He would shake, he would perspire, he would foam at the mouth. Whether they were epileptic or even demonic, he claimed he then received revelations from an angel of light. What were the revelations? They were written down into what is known as the Koran, the Islamic holy book. However, they were not written down until years later because Muhammad himself was uneducated and probably did not even know how to write.[13]

This angel could not have been an angel from heaven because of what it said. Its teachings, as written down, violate the Word of God. All of our spiritual experiences must be verified by God's Word. If there is a new revelation, it must agree with God's oldest revelation, found in the Bible.

False teachers, though less influential than Joseph Smith or Muhammad, exist in many churches today. These people add or take away from the Scriptures and persuade many to follow their heretical or aberrational teaching. Their motives are impure, and their "inspiration" comes from Satan and his demonic forces. Jim Jones, who was responsible for the Jonestown massacre in Guyana, often used the Bible to teach his followers. David Koresh, leader of the Branch Davidian group in Texas, frequently preached from the Scriptures in expounding his ideas.

It is no wonder that Paul calls false teachers "wolves in sheep's clothing." They are convincing, intimidating, persuasive, and wicked.

The apostles and disciples of Jesus boldly rebuked the false teachers who tried to distract and deceive the early church. Peter (Acts 2:14–41; 3:12–26; 4:8–12) and Stephen (Acts 6:8–10; 7:1–60) spoke boldly against the Jews who didn't believe their message. Paul spoke against the Jewish leaders in the cities he visited (Acts 13:16–46; 14:1–4; 17:1–4) and defended his faith in their synagogues. Throughout the history of the Christian church, God has raised up men and women to defend the faith from false teachers. Some of these courageous people are little remembered today:

Quadratus, bishop of Athens, and Aristedes, philosopher of Athens, who wrote a defense of Christianity addressed to Emperor Hadrian about 117 A.D.

Hegesippus, who, between 117 and 138 A.D., wrote about the heresies of Simeon, Cleobus, Gorthoeus, Masbotheus, Menander, Marcion, Carpocrates, Valentinus, Basilides, and Saturnilius, and also the Jewish heresies of the Essenes, Galileans, Hemereobabtists, Samaritans, Sadducees, and Pharisees

Justin Martyr, who wrote his first apology to Emperor Antonius Pius about 138 A.D.

Tatian, who wrote against the Greeks about 163 A.D.

Melito of Sardis, who wrote a discourse to Emperor Antonius around 166 A.D.

During this same period, Musanus Modestus, a disciple of Justin, wrote an elegant work to some of the brothers in the church who had abandoned the truth in favor of the heresy of Encratites and Tatianus. Between 170 and 220, Irenaeus, bishop of Lyons, wrote his famous *Against Heresies,* also known as the *Detection and Overthrow of Falsely-named Knowledge.*[14]

Others who defended the faith from false teachers in the second century A.D. were Rhoto, a disciple of Tatian; Miltiades, from Asia Minor; Apollinius of Rome; Serapion, bishop of Antioch; and Tertullian. Then came the great church fathers of the third century such as Clement of Alexandria, Origen, and Cyprian of Carthage.

The church councils of Antioch (268), Arles (314), and Nicea (325) were called to deal with heresy.

We could go on, because in every age in the history of the church there were people raised up to speak out against false teachers and those who would distract, distort, and deceive.

Protecting Ourselves from False Teachers

HOW CAN WE PROTECT ourselves from false teachers? How can we feel protected physically against the enemy's attack? Protection comes through understanding the truth. Jesus is the way, *the truth,* and the life. He will not let sincere Christians get off track for very long. He will steer them back into the right path.

We must understand the critical importance of knowing the Word of God. David asked, "How can a young man keep his way pure?" and gave the response, "By living according to your word" (Ps. 119:9). He also said, "Your word is a lamp unto my feet and a light for my path" (v. 105). Knowing the truth of Jesus Christ and knowing God's Word are the best safeguard we can have in this world. Jesus told His disciples, "Do not be afraid of those who kill the body but cannot kill the soul" (Matt. 10:28).

It is possible that some who read this book will suffer martyrdom. At this time we in the United States do not commonly suffer death for our faith—but it could happen. A primary threat in America at this time is false teaching and apathy toward the things of God. However, if physical threats come because of our faith, we are not to fear but to trust God with all our hearts. If we suffer because of our testimony, we will be saved in the end. Our physical life does not end on this earth. We go on living in Christ.

A few years ago, missionary statesman Dr. J. Philip Hogan visited Lima, Peru, as a speaker at a national ministers' meeting. The city was in much turmoil and he was warned about possible danger, but Dr. Hogan was sincerely blessed by his weekend of teaching. He closed his last service and began hugging the people and saying good-bye.

Person after person said, while embracing him, "If they shoot us in our churches we will be happy. We want the world to know what we will die for."

Others told Dr. Hogan, "I will see you on the other side."

Dr. Hogan thought that hearing this over and over had to be more than coincidental, so when it was time for him to leave the city, he asked one of the leaders, "Why did many of the people say, 'I will see you on the other side' or 'We want the world to know what we will die for'?"

The answer came back, "All of these national workers are under great physical threat and have suffered much persecution. They truly feel that they could lose their lives at any time."

Before a year passed, more than forty of the national workers had been killed. Although they had suffered the death of martyrs, the work they started remains.

The Battle comes at us on several fronts. Satan will use deception, false teachers who look like "angels of light," intimidation, and physical threats. However, we are not to fear, because the Battle has already been won!

PART TWO

OUR SPIRITUAL WEAPONS

Six

Preparing for Battle

For six generations Sharon's family had been involved in witch-craft. She grew up attending séances, praying to Satan, and performing demonic rites. Involvement in the occult was normal to her, and the frequent paranormal experiences of the spirit world were part of everyday life.

Although Sharon thought that the demonic activity was what life is all about, she was empty inside. She was very aware of her need for answers to life's questions. She increasingly felt more and more oppressed and tormented. Little did she know that what she perceived as a "normal" spirit world was really a world controlled by an unseen power who was out to deceive and ultimately destroy her. Her emotions were out of balance, her thinking was confused, and her life seemed hopeless. She was only in her early twenties, yet she had already experienced most of the destructive things life had to offer. To all appearance she looked like any other young adult—except that her eyes betrayed her fear and confusion.

Sharon knew of a small church near her home. The pastor was young, sincere, and eager to do all he could do to reach his com-munity for Christ. Sharon scheduled an appointment. After dis-covering Sharon's deep involvement in witchcraft, the pastor decided to fast and pray and ask some of his family and friends to do so also before he met with her again.

The pastor sought the Lord and prayed for spiritual power and wisdom to deal with this demonic stronghold. He discerned that her problems arose from her involvement in the occult and a lifestyle that had been in her family for generations. He knew that God could deliver her.

The young pastor had not had this experience before, but he had studied the Bible accounts relating how Jesus and the apostles had prayed for people who were demon possessed. He believed he could do the same as they did.

When Sharon arrived for her next appointment, she was obviously distressed. She wondered, *What am I doing here? This person will not be able to give me any answers.* Amid her tension, she felt that she wanted to run from his office, but deep down inside she somehow knew that this man could help her.

The young pastor greeted her, "Sharon I'm glad you decided to ask for assistance with your problem. With God's help, I believe that we can find some answers for you."

She was visibly tense and uneasy, shifting continually in her chair. Hesitantly she said, "I'm not sure if you can help me. This has been going on for a long time."

"How long, Sharon?"

"For generations," she mumbled.

The pastor's heart went out to this desperate young woman. Calmly but boldly he said, "Sharon, I want to pray for you. I have been praying and fasting for you for several days. I have also asked my wife and some friends to pray, and they are praying for you right now. We believe that God will free you from the oppression and bondage you are feeling. Can I pray for you right now?"

Sharon was silent for a few seconds, then said, "Please help me!"

With quiet authority the pastor began to pray in the name of Jesus. "Satan, I command you and your demonic strongholds to leave Sharon! You have now lost your control and power over this woman and in the name of Jesus Christ, I command you to leave her."

Sharon said she felt some sense of relief, then suddenly cried out, "I know Pastor Miller."

She said in another voice, "I drove Pastor Miller from his church."[1]

The young pastor was surprised at Sharon's words. He knew whom she was talking about and wondered how she could know this pastor, whom she had never met? He thought, *How could she have made him leave his church?*

The pastor continued to pray for Sharon's deliverance. "Devil, leave her in the name of Jesus! With the authority of Jesus Christ I command you to remove any power you have over Sharon!"

Suddenly, Sharon was released. She knew something had happened because she felt a sense of peace and the oppression was gone. Her features relaxed, and the fear was gone from her eyes. Her voice became normal, and she felt a tremendous sense of freedom.

The pastor perceived that Sharon had been delivered, and he immediately instructed her on how to become a Christian. He explained that giving her life over to Jesus Christ was the only way to protect herself from the torment and oppression she had lived with.

"Sharon, God has set you free from the bondage and oppression you have felt for so long. Now you need to protect yourself by giving your life to Jesus Christ. He will never leave you, and He will be there if this demonic spirit comes back to bother you."

Sharon did give her life to Jesus Christ. At this writing, she has been serving the Lord for many months. There have been times of difficulty and times when she felt under attack from the spirit world that she had turned her back on. But she is growing in the grace and peace of God.

The pastor later asked Sharon how she had been involved with Pastor Miller's church. She said that people in the occult sometimes try to curse or pray against powerful churches and Christian leaders.

This kind of story has undoubtedly been repeated many times and in different ways. Many people are unaware of the evil spirit world that would deceive and ultimately destroy them. They may become fascinated and naïvely play around with the paranormal: palm readers, "fortune-telling" 900 phone numbers, astrology and

horoscopes, Ouija boards, channelers, and occultic books. Learning that Sharon had actively prayed against a pastor she had never
met, as well as his church, awakened me to the devious ways by
which the devil and his fallen angels want to prevent Christians
and churches from advancing Christ before a needy world.

The Seven Sons of Sceva

THE BIBLE TELLS A story that has much in common with Sharon's.

> Some Jews who went around driving out evil spirits tried to
> invoke the name of the Lord Jesus over those who were
> demon-posessed. They would say, "In the name of Jesus
> whom Paul preaches, I command you to come out." Seven
> sons of Sceva, a Jewish chief priest, were doing this. The evil
> spirit answered them, "Jesus I know and Paul I know about,
> but who are you?" Then the man who had the evil spirit
> jumped on them and overpowered them all. He gave them
> such a beating that they ran out of the house naked and
> bleeding (Acts 19:13–15).

The demon knew of Jesus and Paul, but it did not know the
young men who were trying to cast it out of "the man." The evil
spirit understood that the seven men had no power over it because
they were not Christians. The demon-possessed man attacked
them and ripped their clothes off.

We learn from this biblical account that demons know who
Jesus is and they also know the people who have given their lives
to Jesus Christ. They are aware that Christians have power over
them and that non-Christians do not.

When the pastor confronted the evil spirit in Sharon's life, he
was victorious because he knew Jesus Christ and had the wisdom
to pray for strength and knowledge to deal with the demon. When
the sons of Sceva confronted the evil spirit in Corinth, they were
unsuccessful because they had no relationship with Jesus. They
were a mockery to the demon that lived in this man.

God did not create us to lose the spiritual battles we experience in life. All of us experience satanic conflict, and all of us can

develop strengths that will enable us to be consistently victorious in our walk with the Lord. There is no attack from the enemy of our souls so strong that God cannot give us the insight and strength we need to resist. In our unique spiritual journeys there are three attitudes we must acquire that will prepare us for battle, no matter what Satan throws our way.

Gaining Confidence

WE MUST BELIEVE THAT we have authority in the spiritual realm because of what Jesus Christ did for us. Jesus clearly demonstrated authority over the demonic world when He was on earth, and He has passed this authority on to those who follow Him. When we become Christians we become dead to the old nature (Rom. 6:11; 1 Cor. 15:31) and alive to Christ. The same resurrection power that raised Jesus Christ from the dead dwells in Christians (see Ephesians 1:19–20). Paul tells the church at Colosse, "He has rescued us from the dominion of darkness and brought us into the kingdom of the Son he loves" (Col. 1:13).

Just imagine a military officer being hesitant in his leadership when he knows he has all the power he needs to win the battle. He can have all the personnel, all the weaponry, and a creative strategy for the battlefront, but if the enemy notices a lack of confidence and takes advantage of his hesitancy, the well-equipped officer will suffer serious damage because of his indecision.

We need to understand that God will protect His children, but we must have confidence in His ability not only to protect us but also to enable us to win in spiritual warfare. We are not alone. Jesus will be with us—always—and we can trust that He will help us. Before He left the earth, Jesus told his disciples, "I will not leave you as orphans; I will come to you" (John 14:18). He said, "I will ask the Father, and he will give you another Counselor to be with you forever" (v. 16). We can have confidence that just as Jesus walked with the early disciples, the Holy Spirit will walk with us today. In the same way that Jesus taught and demonstrated spiritual power with those early believers, so the Holy Spirit will teach us how to use the authority God has given every believer. Our confidence comes because of who Jesus Christ is and what He did for us. Our ever-present helper is the Holy Spirit (see John 14:26).

Confidence will grow in our lives. As we decide to use the gifts God has given us and rely on His protection, we will experience victory after victory in the spiritual life. Soon we will be able to look back and see how God has helped us win on major battlefronts.

Developing Courage

WHEN VISITING THE BEAUTIFUL city of Bangkok, Thailand, a few years ago, I and the group of Christians with me took a tour of some religious temples. I had done some study on the various Eastern religious traditions common in that part of the world. As we walked around the temple in one particular village, I noted, "Look at how the people need to repaint their gods—they are actually falling apart before their eyes!" I told the group that many of the idols we were observing were the "actual" gods they worshiped. We saw numerous people crying out to these gods who could not hear, see, understand, or answer them. This only made us more eager to tell these people about our God, who constantly hears our petitions, answers our cries, and cares about His children.

As I was giving a very limited lesson about the temple we were visiting, I noticed a Buddhist monk walking across the patio toward us. Seeing him, I felt a strange sensation. I sensed that he was going to try to deceive someone in my group and demonstrate occultic power, but I temporarily dismissed this thought as a figment of my imagination.

When he was a few feet away, the monk greeted us in English. "Hello! Are you visiting our country from America?"

Several in the group smiled and said, "Yes, we have just arrived."

I felt impressed to take control of the conversation and said, "You have a beautiful country, and it is an honor to visit."

The monk looked directly at one of the people in the group and smugly said, "I can tell you where you were born and your mother's name."

We were stunned. I felt a boldness come over me, and I responded, "I will not permit you to do that, and in the name of Jesus Christ I rebuke the power that gives you this ability!"

The monk was silent for a few seconds, surprised by my direct confrontation. Gathering his thoughts, he said, "I have the gift of knowing great details about people's lives. Why would you try to stop me from giving this gift?"

I said, "The power you have to do this is not from heaven. It is demonic, and I come against that demonic activity."

Again the monk looked bewildered. He did not seem to understand. He responded, "I have never had this type of experience or seen such authority. I have studied my religion for over fifteen years and am an expert with its practice. Who is your God, and how can you have such power?"

The small group of believers stood by amazed during this conversation and were eagerly awaiting my answer.

"My Lord and my God is Jesus Christ. He is the true power and authority over all the spirit world. The Bible, which my God has given us, commands that we do not become acquainted with other false gods. You can know my God, too."

I held my New Testament out to him and said, "This is a portion of His book."

Even though he was dressed in monk's clothing, with his head shaved, and displayed a very religious demeanor, I could see spiritual hunger in his eyes as I talked. He said, "I want to know more about your God. Will that book tell me about Him?"

I said, "Yes, this book will tell you about Him. Here, you can have my book." I handed my New Testament to him, and he gratefully accepted it. I then said, "Sir, you can become a Christian right now. You do not need to study this book but only to surrender your life to Jesus Christ."

Softly he replied, "I want to study your book, and then I will make a decision." He excused himself and left.[2]

The amazing thing about this story is that I am sure the monk *could* have named the birthdate and mother's name of the person he was talking to. The Holy Spirit had warned me that the monk would try to deceive someone in our group. His small supernatural demonstration would have brought confusion to the young believers. This confrontation was a face-off in the spirit world. And the Holy Spirit gave direction and courage to win.

When Joshua was about to lead the children of Israel into the Promised Land, God told him over and over again, "Be strong and of good courage" (Josh. 1:6, 9, 18). We can have faith, confidence, and trust, but we must all come to the point of decision. We must step out by faith. Every spiritual advance in the history of the church has required courage, a courage that says, "With God's help we can do this!"

When the Christians in the early church were threatened, imprisoned, and warned not to speak or teach in the name of Jesus, they had a prayer meeting. I am sure they were concerned and wondered what they should do. Should they keep quiet? Should they go underground with their faith? They said among themselves, "We cannot keep quiet about what God has done for us and what He wants to do for everyone!" They prayed, "Now, Lord, consider their threats and enable your servants to speak your word with great boldness" (Acts 4:29). And what happened? "After they prayed, the place where they were meeting was shaken. And they were all filled with the Holy Spirit and spoke the word of God boldly" (v. 31).

Those early Christians did not stop when they were opposed, and we must not stop, either. God will give us the courage to fight whatever battles the enemy involves us in.

Relying on God

WE CANNOT WIN THIS battle alone. We need God's help. Some Christians boast of having great power or authority, but we should become concerned when they give that impression. Our attitude should be, We can do all things "through Christ"! Not through our ability, but rather our availability to Him. We cannot put our confidence in our own strength; we must trust and rely on Him to win the battle for us. Even Jesus demonstrated great trust and humility before His Father. He was continually doing His Father's will. When we are in spiritual battle we need to look to the Lord, pray, and humbly trust that He will help us win.

Christians must depend on the Lord for everything in their lives, including spiritual battles. We no longer belong to ourselves but are under new ownership. Jesus Christ paid the price for us and will defend us as we depend on Him for victory. Our total reliance is on Him. We do not need to be afraid that the devil will surprise and attack us at any time. We can rely on the fact that Jesus will help us in everything. As we walk our journey through life, living for God and seeking ways to care for, teach, and help people, we can be sure that the enemy will attack and try to distract us. Our focus should not be on what the devil might do, but on the truth that Jesus will help us no matter what happens.

On many occasions we may meet Christians who are constantly looking for the devil or his demons. We have seen people cast demons out of rooms, buildings, cities, nations, and more. Their focus is on what the devil might do. But in Scripture we see the people of God concerned about what the Lord can do, not what the devil is trying to do. Our eyes are to be fixed on Jesus, and our passion is to do His will. We need to have an understanding that as long as we are living in the will of God, the enemy will try to throw us off course. Yet, our God will be there on every occasion. He will never abandon us. He will help us to be well-equipped soldiers.

Billy Graham said,

> Spiritual forces and resources are available to all Christians. Because our resources are unlimited, Christians will be winners. Millions of angels are at God's command and at our service. The hosts of heaven stand at attention as we make our way from earth to glory, and Satan's BB guns are no match for God's heavy artillery. So don't be afraid. God is for you. He has committed his angels to wage war in the conflict of the ages—and they will win the victory.[3]

In his book *What Works,* Stuart Briscoe writes, "The fact of the matter is that I take refuge in the Lord. Unashamedly I run to

Him. In fact, if it were not for the ready access I have to Him, I would never survive the ministry. The pressures would be more that I could take. I hide myself away with Him. I crawl into a corner and talk to Him. When the pressure is on, I pull the drapes and commune with Him. I take refuge in Him."[4]

We, too, can rely on God and trust Him to help us win every spiritual battle.

SEVEN ⤟

Our Victorious Conqueror

World War II had been over for sixteen years, yet in the jungles, caves, and hill country of Guam a confused Japanese soldier was still in hiding. He defied capture and refused to surrender, mentally fighting a war that was over for his comrades almost two decades before. He did not know that World War II had ended, with his country going down in defeat.

Because of periodic sightings, there was some suspicion that a few Japanese soldiers could be left on the island of two-hundred-plus square miles. While Sergeant Ito Masashi was climbing over a rock near the American camp one day, the inevitable finally happened. He knew he was spotted. He froze. He thought he would be slaughtered when captured. Hoping there was a small chance that his life would be spared, he held a square of old trouser material in the air as an act of surrender.

Ito later wrote, "Now that the moment of truth had come; now that I was finally face to face, after sixteen years, with the enemy we had always dreaded, curiously I felt no panic, no fear. I watched almost dispassionately as one of the quartet detached himself and advanced down the slope toward me. I'd no time to wonder if he was going to kill me then and there—for an instant later I was engulfed, swamped, overwhelmed by a shock and a surprise as heart-stopping as anything I'd experienced in my whole life."[1]

Ito braced himself for whatever might happen, but one of the men approached him gently and said, "You're all right now, are you?"[2] There would be no slaughter, no darkness, no pain. They had compassion. He was given medical attention and hygiene care. (His hair had grown to almost two feet in length, and dirt was literally crusted on his body.) Ito was given a warm shower, fitted with new clothing, and given conventional food. In a short time he was flown back to his family in Japan, who thought he had died years before. At home his tombstone read, "Killed in action on Guam Island, at the age of twenty-three."[3]

The story of Sergeant Masashi reminds us of the condition of most of the people in the world today. They are unaware that a "spiritual war" was fought and that the battle was won when Christ went to the cross two thousand years ago. Many people are so harassed, confused, and tormented by the activity of Satan that they live only for today—they just want to get by. So many live in fear of what they perceive to be inevitable, namely, that life will become hard and cruel. These people have given in to the idea that they will never really find the answers they are looking for.

After a recent speaking engagement, I was approached by a woman in her thirties who wanted to speak to me. Her little girl, who appeared to be five or six years old, gazed affectionately at her as the woman, whom we'll call Kim, told me her shocking story. For more than eight months Kim had been living on the streets. Her daughter was living with a relative, and her twelve-year-old son was in a juvenile detention facility. Kim said that her father had severely beaten her while she was growing up and, as a result, she began developing relationships with men who abused her as well. She had suffered numerous rapes and severe beatings.

Kim cried out to me, "Where was God in all this? Why did this have to happen to me? Life hasn't been fair! While living on the streets I tried praying, and anything else I could do to turn my life around, but nothing worked."

Now her life was beginning to "work," and she didn't fully understand. Kim had just recently accepted Christ and was gaining some hope that her future would be different. But she had become discouraged. She said, "Maybe I should just go back to what I know life is all about—back to the people who abused me. That seems to be my life."

I said, "Kim, look at that little girl holding your hand. She adores you and wants you to be a mom to her. Because of your recent decision to become a Christian, Jesus has broken the power of sin in your life. The chain of bondage has been severed. And because of your decision, this little girl will not suffer the kind of life you have had."

Kim responded, "I know you're right. I just don't know if it will work. I've lived that other life for so long, and there are so many bad memories."

"I understand your fear and your apprehension about the future," I said, "but as you grow in the Lord and as He helps you settle down, you will see that He has a wonderful life for you and your children."

Kim has gotten involved in her church, and a Christian counselor is helping her work through her painful past. She is going to make it.[4]

The enemy of our souls has been very thorough in his work of keeping people blind to what Jesus did for them on the cross. Many people, even in churches, do not fully comprehend all that Jesus did when He died.

At times people even mock the crucifixion of Jesus. Some rock songs do this. In the Rolling Stones' song "Sympathy for the Devil," Mick Jagger sings, "I was around when Jesus Christ had His moment of doubt and pain, made [expletive deleted] sure that Pilate washed his hands and sealed His fate."

John Lennon of the Beatles said, "Christianity will go. It will vanish and shrink. I needn't argue about that. I'm right, and I will be proved right. We're more popular than Jesus."[5] The arrogance of Jagger, Lennon, and many of their counterparts proves that they have absolutely no idea what they are talking about. Eric Holmberg, who directs Real-to-Reel Ministries, has produced a video on what many contemporary rock music "philosophers" are saying about Jesus Christ. Holmberg states, "Jesus has become the focus of more ridicule in rock music than any other personality. Virtually every facet of His life and ministry is mocked and criticized."[6] Noting that many rock stars like to wear a cross as jewelry, Holmberg says,

> How Satan must enjoy the irony. This type of desecration is virtually rampant in rock. With crosses the most popular jewelry choice of the stars, it seems as though the more perverted the artist, the larger, the more numerous or the more obsessive is their focus on the cross. . . . Crosses show up so often you would think that rock music was a Christian industry—until one looks at their intent, message, and lifestyle.[7]

What these rock musicians and most of the world do not realize is that the age-old conflict between God and the devil was finished on that ridiculed "old rugged cross." According to the Bible, there will come a day when rock stars such as Mick Jagger, John Lennon, and Madonna will acknowledge that Jesus Christ is Lord and that and the cross is the greatest demonstration of God's love and victory that history has ever known.

The effects of the crucifixion will one day be felt by everyone who has ever lived.

In his classic book *Mere Christianity*, C. S. Lewis illustrates this truth:

> This universe is at war. . . . it is a civil war, a rebellion. . . . we are living in a part of the universe occupied by the rebel.
> Enemy-occupied territory—that is what this world is. Christianity is the story of how the rightful king has landed, you might say landed in disguise, and is calling us all to take part in a great campaign of sabotage. When you go to church you are really listening-in to the secret wireless [radio] from our friends: that is why the enemy is so anxious to prevent us from going. He does it by playing on our conceit and laziness and intellectual snobbery.[8]

What Happened When Jesus Died?

PAUL PAINTS A VIVID word picture of a public execution to explain the absolute victory Jesus had over Satan when he suffered and died on the cross. If we understand the significance of this event, our confidence for battle with the enemy will greatly increase. Paul writes,

> When you were dead in your sins and in the uncircumcision of your sinful nature, God made you alive with Christ. He forgave us all our sins, having canceled the written code, with its regulations, that was against us and that stood opposed to us; he took it away, nailing it to the cross. And having disarmed the powers and authorities, he made a public spectacle of them, triumphing over them by the cross (Col. 2:13–15).

Three major truths derive from this passage that we need to understand as we prepare for spiritual warfare:

Jesus gave us new life. When we come to Christ, we come alive. This new life is a gift from God and is what the Scripture means that calls us to be "born again" (John 3:3, 7). With this new life we have broken away from our past. We have been "set free from sin" (Rom. 6:18). Before we came to Christ we were hopelessly bankrupt in our sins and had no chance of getting out of spiritual debt. But on the cross the debt was canceled. We can say, "Jesus took the document that revealed our sins and, in public defiance to the powers of evil, He nailed it to the cross. On that day almost two thousand years ago, Christ paid in full all of our sin debt."

Arthur Stanton said, "We are not saved by theories, but by fact, and what is the fact? For whom did Christ die? Christ died for sinners. Well, then, He died for me."[9] The great statesman Daniel Webster said, "If I might comprehend Jesus Christ, I could not believe on Him. He would be no greater than myself. Such is my consciousness of sin and inability that I must have a superhuman Savior."[10]

The employees at the Assemblies of God headquarters have a chapel service every Tuesday morning. After one recent service, a man I had not met asked to speak to me.[11] He said he would be going to his attorney's office that day to sign divorce papers. His wife had worked at our headquarters facility as a secretary. They had not lived together for many months. He said that for some reason he felt that he should drive by the building and come in—and he did, during the chapel service. He sat outside the meeting room and heard the singing, the prayers, and the message.

As the man talked to me, he began to cry. "I don't know what's the matter," he said. "I have a good wife and beautiful children. My life is a mess. I used to be a Christian, but I began to use drugs and alcohol, and I became very confused. Then, I got involved in all kinds of bad behavior."

I said, "Tell me how this all started."

He responded, "I stopped going to church, and in fact tried to keep my wife and kids away from church. My wife was strong, and she decided to attend on her own, with the kids."

"When did you leave her, and what made you decide to divorce her?" I asked.

"I lost my job, and my life just got more messed up. I decided it was better for me to leave the family—they would be better off without me. I have done so many things wrong, God couldn't ever forgive me."

I responded, "Friend, Jesus already paid for your debt of sin. You can receive His forgiveness right now and start over again. With God's help, you can stop the pattern of sin, and perhaps your family will even be willing to start over, too. God is the God of the second chance."

The man asked me to pray with him. With heartfelt sobs he confessed his sins and re-dedicated his life to Christ. I called his wife at her office to tell her that her husband was in the chapel, praying. She immediately came down, and they sat, talked, and prayed together. She didn't want a divorce—and most of all, the sin debt was paid for.

This man, like countless others, has discovered the amazing truth that *all* our sins have been covered. We need only to accept the gift of salvation.

Jesus canceled the written code that was against us. Jesus Christ canceled not only our debt of sin—for sins we know that we have committed—but also the sins based on the regulations of the law. To understand what this means, we can look at two of the original Greek words Paul used.

Written code. The Greek word *cheirographon* literally means handwriting. It refers to a signature agreeing to an indebtedness. If we want to buy an automobile and finance it through a bank, we will sign a document stating that we understand that we owe a certain amount of money to the bank and that the loan will be paid over a period of time at an agreed-upon interest rate. Our signature states that we understand the conditions of the agreement and that if we do not meet those conditions, we could lose the car, and have a negative mark on our credit rating.

Paul is saying that people understand that they have a debt of sin. The Bible teaches us, "There is no one righteous, not even one" (Rom. 3:10). We know we have done many things that God could hold against us—whether they be horrendous sins or an "everyday" kind. But we all know there is a sin debt that somehow needs to be paid. How do we know? Our "consciences" bear witness, and our "thoughts" are accusing (Rom. 2:15). In our hearts we have signed an agreement that we have a sin debt.

Canceled (exaleiphein). Paul then explains that this debt of sin has been canceled, or wiped out. God has mercifully paid the entire debt. In explaining the word *exaleiphein*, William Barclay writes,

> The substance on which ancient documents were written was either papyrus, a kind of paper made of the pith of the bulrush, or vellum, a substance made of the skins of animals. Both were fairly expensive and certainly could not be wasted. Ancient ink had no acid in it; it lay on the surface of the paper and did not, as modern ink usually does, bite into it. Sometimes a scribe, to save paper, used papyrus or vellum that had already been written upon. When he did that, he took a sponge and wiped the writing out. Because it was only on the surface of the paper, the ink could be wiped out as if it had never been.[12]

When we receive the forgiveness of God, the slate is wiped clean. It is so complete that there is no record of any debt. "You will again have compassion on us; you will tread our sins underfoot and hurl all our iniquities into the depths of the sea" (Micah 7:19). In the same way, David writes, "As far as the east is from the west, so far has he removed our transgressions from us" (Ps. 103:12).

A computer has a delete button that will remove whatever the user has highlighted. We could work all day on a document, but if we hit the delete button, it will all disappear. All that we have worked on will be removed. God in His incredible mercy has wiped our slate clean of sin. The sins we have committed were highlighted, and the delete button was hit at the moment we came to Christ for His forgiveness. This new "file" is now stored in place of the old. In Christ our sins are completely forgiven. We are "free from accusation—if you continue in your faith" (Col. 1:22–23). Evangelist Billy Zeoli said, "God has a big eraser."[13]

In his personal memoirs Charles Finney expresses his emotions when, in 1821, he finally realized that his sins were forgiven.

> But how was I to account for the quiet of my mind? I tried to recall my convictions, to get back again the load of sin under which I had been laboring. But all sense of sin, all consciousness of present sin or guilt, had departed from me. I said to myself, "What is this, that I cannot arouse any sense of guilt in my soul, as great a sinner as I am?" I tried in vain to make myself anxious about my present state. I was so quiet and peaceful that I tried to feel concerned about that, lest it should be a result of my having grieved the Spirit away. But take any view of it I would, I could not be anxious at all about my soul, and about my spiritual state. The repose of my mind was unspeakably great. I never can describe it in words. The thought of God was sweet to my mind, and the most profound spiritual tranquillity had taken full possession of me.[14]

What a wonderful experience Finney had when he actually sensed in his emotions the truth that he was completely forgiven. Not all of us will have that kind of emotional experience, but we can always depend on God's promise, "If we confess our sins, he is faithful and just and will forgive us our sins and purify us from all unrighteousnes" (1 John 1:9). God's Word is true, no matter what our emotions tell us.

Further on this matter of cancellation, Paul states that the written code was nailed to the cross (Col. 2:13). That is, God took our sins and nailed them to the cross of Christ.

Barclay writes,

> It used to be said that in the ancient world when a law or an ordinance was canceled, it was fastened to a board and a nail was driven clean through it. But it is doubtful if that was the case and if that is the picture here. Rather it is this—on the cross of Christ the indictment that was against us was itself crucified. It was executed and put clean out of the way, so that it might never be seen again.[15]

Before Christ, people were under the law and found they could not keep it perfectly. They were continually breaking the law on one point or another. But with the cross the law has been canceled and God's grace has come.[16]

C. I. Scofield once wrote,

> God was not changed, for He had always loved the world; nor was the world changed, for it continued in sinful rebellion against God. But by the death of Christ the relationship between God and the world was changed.[17]

Thomas Drake said, "The cross is the ladder to heaven."[18]

What sins have you committed? Do you have a habit of lying? A recent poll disclosed that in the opinion of Americans, the clergy tell the truth 49 percent of the time, doctors 48 percent, best friends 26 percent, local newspapers 8 percent, the president of the United States 8 percent, and leaders of Congress 3 percent. Yet most adults would say that they do not lie and value personal integrity.[19] Perhaps your sin has been cheating, adultery, pornography, gossip, slander, envy, or anger. The type of sin makes little difference to God. Sin can be forgiven, because our sins have been nailed to the cross. By acknowledging our sin to God and asking Him for forgiveness, we can receive His cleansing.

Jesus disarmed all the demonic forces that take people captive. In regard to Paul's words in Colossians 2:15—"having disarmed the powers and authorities, he made a public spectacle of them"—Barclay comments,

> The ancient world believed in all kinds of angels and in all kinds of elemental spirits. Many of these spirits were out to ruin men. It was they who were responsible for demon-possession and the like. They were hostile to men. Jesus conquered them forever. He stripped them; the word used is the word for stripping the weapons and the armor from a defeated foe. Once and for all Jesus broke their power. He put them to open shame and led them captive in his triumphant train. The picture is that of the triumph of a Roman general. When a Roman general had won a really notable victory, he was allowed to march his victorious armies through the streets of Rome and behind him followed the kings and the leaders and the peoples he had vanquished. They were openly branded as his spoils. Paul thinks of Jesus as a conqueror enjoying a kind of cosmic triumph, and in his triumphal procession are the powers of evil, beaten forever, for every one to see.[20]

The demonic forces understand that once we have been forgiven in Christ they can no longer control us. Their ability to keep us in darkness is gone, and even their influence on us has been greatly damaged. Jesus disarmed them and publicly displayed their defeat.

What Did We Gain from the Cross?

PAUL WRITES, "FOR HE has rescued us from the dominion of darkness and brought us into the kingdom of the Son he loves. In whom we have redemption, the forgiveness of sins" (Col. 1:13). The work that Jesus Christ accomplished on the cross has many benefits that directly affect our spiritual warfare.

We have been rescued from Satan's kingdom. When we become born again we are rescued from Satan's dominion and brought into the kingdom of God. The Greek word translated "brought" is *methistemi,* which means to transport something or someone completely over to another place. As Christians we are no longer part of Satan's kingdom. We might occasionally do things we did when we lived in that kingdom, but we are not a part of it. We have been rescued. We have been transferred.

We have been delivered from darkness. When we were without Christ, we were blind, without hope, and stumbling around looking for answers to life's questions. Now we live in the light, and Jesus leads us where we are to go. We are children of God, not children of the devil.

Dr. James Dobson explains our basic sin nature this way:

> Many people believe that children are basically good, and they only learn to do wrong from their parents and culture. But if that assessment of human nature were accurate, it would contradict scriptural understandings. For Jeremiah wrote: "The heart is deceitful above all things, and desperately wicked: who can know it?" (Jeremiah 17:9 KJV). Jeremiah's inspired insight into human nature is validated by the sordid history of mankind. The path of civilization is blotted by murder, war, rape, and plundering—from the time of Adam forward.
>
> This record of evil makes it difficult to hold the view that children are pure and holy at birth. Greed, lust, and selfishness characterize us all. Is this nature also evident in children? King David thought so, for he confessed, "in sin did my mother conceive me" (Psalm 51:5 KJV).
>
> What meaningful difference, then, is made by the distinction between the two views of children? Practically everything! Parents who believe all toddlers are infused with goodness and sunshine are encouraged to get out of the way and let their pleasant natures unfold.
>
> Parents who recognize the inevitable internal war between good and evil will do their best to influence the child's choices—to shape his will and provide a solid spiritual

foundation. They acknowledge the dangers of adult defiance as expressed in 1 Samuel 15:23: "For rebellion is as the sin of witchcraft, and stubbornness is as worshipping idols" (TLB).[21]

The predominate desire of Satan is to control. Before we came to Christ, Satan had tremendous ability to influence us to do his will because of the condition of our hearts and because we were part of his domain. Once we had yielded to his desires, we became captive—habitual offenders—to a corrupt mind-set and behavior patterns. By ourselves it was impossible to break free.

Occasionally people seeking pastoral help have said, "I don't want to do what I am doing. I can't seem to get free of it." They might be addicted to alcohol, drugs, cursing, smoking, pornography, sexual perversions, or thinking patterns that continually depress them. There is a struggle for control going on. These people are living in darkness.

God has raised up many professional Christian counselors who are a gift to the body of Christ for the help they provide. However, it takes more than commonsense advice or refined counseling techniques to set people free from Satan's control. Only Jesus Christ can do that. Christian counselors need to utilize this truth as they endeavor to help people.

We have been set free from sin. When we are converted to Christ, Satan's control is broken. F. F. Bruce writes, "This redemption was procured by Christ for His people once for all, but it is received by them individually as they become united with Him by faith."[22] On countless occasions people have suddenly become free of devastating and tyrannical behavior patterns at the moment of coming to Christ. They have experienced this miracle because they are a part of God's kingdom now.

It seems that everywhere we turn, people are being transformed and the bondage of sin is being broken as they come to Christ. A tough gang leader named Nicky Cruz, who heard about Jesus through David Wilkerson's ministry in New York City, now preaches the gospel to thousands of young people in crusades throughout the world.

Charles Colson, who was once Richard Nixon's "hatchet man" to do the "President's Dirty Work,"[23] went to jail for Watergate-related crimes. Not long after Colson's life hit bottom, Jesus Christ got ahold of him. Since his conversion Colson has developed an important ministry to prisoners—Prison Fellowship—and has written numerous Christian books.

Jim Elliot and four of his friends went to Ecuador to tell the Auca people about Christ. Within months, the five men were found speared to death along the Curaray River. Kimo and Komi, two men who participated in the massacre, were so affected by the testimony of the men they had killed that they gave their lives to Christ soon after the tragic event. They learned from the witness of these men that Jesus had power over evil spirits.[24]

William J. Murray, who grew up in the home of the famous atheist Madalyn Murray O'Hair, gave his life to Christ while reading the gospel of Luke.[25] D. James Kennedy writes that since that event, Murray "is a powerful evangelist and also an advocate of allowing God back into the public schools—this is the very man who, as a boy, had been at the center of Murray v. Curlett (1963), one of the key Supreme Court school-prayer decisions."[26]

Jeff Fenholt, a former vocalist for the rock group Black Sabbath who played the role of Jesus in the opera *Jesus Christ Superstar*, realized his life was empty, confused, and meaningless. He gave his life to the real Jesus Christ and now sings Christian songs and appears frequently on Christian television programs.[27]

Sy Rogers, a committed homosexual who dressed and acted like a woman for a year and a half, wrote, "Achieving much desired acceptance in my role as a woman, I was considered attractive and even popular in gay circles."[28] Sy knew his life was abnormal and empty. He decided to become a Christian, and with his salvation experience he became free of homosexuality. Sy now helps homosexuals and transsexuals come out of bondage by counseling them to come to Jesus Christ.[29]

We could name countless others who have been unmistakably transformed by the power of God when they gave their lives to Christ.

We have been forgiven. As committed Christians, we are free of accusation. "Therefore, there is now no condemnation for those who are in Christ Jesus" (Rom. 8:1). When our sins are forgiven, we are no longer under the judgment of God. We might remember the sinful things we have done, and the devil might accuse us and try to intimidate us, but we can be as sure as God's inerrant Word that we are no longer condemned.

We belong to Jesus Christ. A transfer has taken place. We are no longer under the ownership of Satan, but belong to Christ.

Many American missionaries travel around the country to raise their budgetary support before they go overseas. Often they also raise funds to build churches or schools or to provide medical services or relief programs. Seldom do the missionaries physically take the funds with them. The money can be transferred by wire from a bank in the United States to a bank in their new country. Once the transfer has been made, no funds remain in the original bank—they are in the new bank and under new management.

Similarly, those who come to Christ have been transferred. Satan no longer has the right, or the ability, to manage people who are not part of his kingdom. We are citizens of the kingdom of God, a kingdom of righteousness, holiness, and light.

Jesus explained to Paul in these terms what his life work would be: "I am sending you to them [the Gentiles] to open their eyes and turn them from darkness to light, and from the power of Satan to God, so that they may receive forgiveness of sins and a place among those who are sanctified by faith in me" (Acts 26:18). Paul was being asked to tell the world what Christ had done for them. They no longer had to live in darkness or be bound by Satan, but could live in the light and be forgiven.

When Christ died on the cross, Satan thought he had finally defeated the Son of God and foiled God's purposes. In his sickening arrogance, however, he lost the battle forever. E. K. Simpson and F. F. Bruce put it this way:

> The very instrument of disgrace and death by which the hostile forces thought they had Him in their grasp and had conquered Him forever was turned by Him into the instrument

of their defeat and captivity. As He was suspended there, bound hand and foot to the wood in apparent weakness, they imagined they had Him at their mercy, and flung themselves upon Him with hostile intent. But, far from suffering their assault without resistance, He grappled with them and mastered them, stripping them of all the armor in which they trusted, and held them aloft in His mighty, out-stretched hands, displaying to the universe their helplessness and His own unvanquished strength. Had they but realized the truth, those "archons of this age"—had they (as Paul puts it in another epistle) known the hidden wisdom of God which decreed the glory of Christ and His people—"They would not have crucified the Lord of glory" (1 Cor 2:8). But now they are disabled and dethroned, and the shameful tree has become the victor's triumphal chariot, before which His captives are driven in humiliating procession, the involuntary and impotent confessors of their overcomer's superiority.[30]

Because of the death, burial, and physical resurrection of Jesus Christ, we can turn from darkness to light. We can be rescued from the power of Satan and come under the control of God. We can be forgiven of the sins that would have condemned us and can become holy. The cross of Jesus Christ changed history for everyone, forever. This cruel execution, which at the time seemed to pass without much notice, became the centerpiece of human civilization past, present, and future. Because of the cross, mankind has hope.

The Battle has been won.

EIGHT ✦

Our Invincible
Armor

If anyone was likely to suffer from an extreme case of battle
fatigue and delayed stress syndrome, it was the apostle Paul.
There is good reason why he has more to say on the subject of
spiritual warfare than any other biblical writer. Simply put, he
experienced it. In a biography of Paul, John Pollock writes,

> The ancient tradition of Paul's execution site is almost
> certainly authentic but the details cannot be fixed. . . . They
> marched him out through the walls past the pyramid of Ces-
> tius which still stands, on to the Ostian Way toward the sea.
> Crowds journeying to or from Ostia would recognize an exe-
> cution squad by the lictors (a Roman Officer) with their
> fasces (a bundle) of Rods and axe, and the executioner car-
> rying a sword, which in Nero's reign had replaced the axe;
> by the escort, and by the manacled criminal, walking stiffly
> and bandy-legged, ragged and filthy from his prison:. . .
>
> He is believed to have been put overnight in a tiny cell,
> for this was a common place of execution. If Luke was
> allowed to stay by his window, if Timothy or Mark had
> reached Rome in time, the sounds of the night vigil would
> not be of weeping but singing: "as sorrowful yet always
> rejoicing; as dying and, behold, we live."
>
> At first light the soldiers took Paul to the pillar. The exe-
> cutioner stood ready, stark naked. Soldiers stripped Paul to
> the waist and tied him, kneeling upright, to the pillar which
> left his neck free. Some accounts say the lictors beat him

with rods; a beating had been the usual prelude to beheading but in recent years not always inflicted. If they must administer this last, senseless dose of pain to a body so soon to die, Who shall separate us from the love of Christ? Shall tribulation . . . or sword?

"I reckon that the sufferings of this present time are not worthy to be compared with"—the flash of a sword—"the glory."[1]

Before his conversion, Saul (later Paul) was one of the greatest persecutors of the early church. He watched the blood flow from Stephen's stone-inflicted wounds. Stephen was perhaps the first Christian martyr (Acts 7:57–58). Before Stephen's death, Saul saw this innocent young man fearlessly look toward heaven and say, "Look, I see heaven open and the Son of Man standing at the right hand of God. . . . Lord, do not hold this sin against them" (vv. 56, 60).

With vicious zeal Saul "began to destroy the church" (Acts 8:3). He went from house to house with the determination of a Gestapo agent, looking for evidence of sedition. To Saul's way of thinking, people who made Jesus "the Nazarene" their Lord were a threat to the Jewish faith and guilty of treason. He would arrest men and women and parade them in front of the high priest, demanding that these Christians curse or deny Jesus. If they would not disclaim their faith they were punished—usually by public flogging—incarcerated, and possibly put to death.

Saul watched and listened to person after person speak of love and commitment to Jesus "the Christ." Some witnessed the flogging of husband or wife, an ordeal worse than their own beating, and perchance they would cry out their agonizing curse on the Jesus they loved. Saul may have shaken his head in disgust over what he perceived as the naïveté of misguided people taken in by a religious sect.

Saul had heard that some of these "who belong to the way" were in Damascus. He received permission from the high priest to go to the synagogue of Damascus, and take these "disciples of Jesus" as prisoners to Jerusalem. While traveling to Damascus, Saul experienced something he had not anticipated.

As he neared Damascus on his journey, suddenly a light from heaven flashed around him. He fell to the ground and heard a voice say to him, "Saul, Saul, why do you persecute me?"

"Who are you, Lord?" Saul asked.

"I am Jesus, whom you are persecuting," he replied (Acts 9:3–5).

Saul knew that the resurrected Jesus had spoken to him. When he opened his eyes he was physically blind but spiritually able to see. He now knew that the Christians were right: Jesus is both savior and Lord. Within a few days Saul was healed of the physical blindness, too. He was filled with the Holy Spirit and was baptized (see vv. 17–18). The persecutor became the preacher, and now *he* became the target of those who wanted to destroy this infant church.

Paul's God-given gifts were many, and over the years his faith grew. This apostle wrote thirteen books of the New Testament, began numerous churches, and mentored countless leaders. He also understood what the weapons of spiritual warfare are. He wrote about spiritual warfare from a deep theological background and personal experience. He wrote,

> Five times I received from the Jews the forty lashes minus one. Three times I was beaten with rods, once I was stoned, three times I was shipwrecked, I spent a night and a day in the open sea. I have been constantly on the move. I have been in danger from rivers, in danger from bandits, in danger from my own countrymen, in danger from Gentiles; in danger in the city, in danger in the country, in danger at sea; and in danger from false brothers. I have labored and toiled and have often gone without sleep; I have known hunger and thirst and have often gone without food; I have been cold and naked (2 Cor. 11:24–27).

What was it that kept Paul going? What kind of strength did he have? What courage? Where did he turn when the enemy's attack seemed bigger than life? He knew there was an invincible armor that God gives to every believer. That armor is only one absolute safeguard against the attack of the enemy.

Pat Robertson reminds us that "Jesus Christ came to destroy all the works of the devil. He has given His disciples power over all the works of the enemy."[2] When the enemy tempts us to moral compromise, we can depend on the armor God has given us. When we are weak emotionally, we can trust that the armor of God will withstand the sniper attack of Satan and his demonic forces. When we wonder whether we have enough spiritual strength, we can rest behind the shield of faith that we have in Christ.

Our heritage and our experiences, as wonderful as they might be, are not a safeguard against the attacks of the enemy. In fact, the Scriptures warn that "if you think you are standing firm, be careful that you don't fall!" (1 Cor. 10:12). Why is that? Because when we think we can win the battle in our own strength and we think we have learned or experienced all that we need, then Satan will take advantage of our pride and come in to blast away and knock us off our feet. Robertson says,

> All men of faith in the church have recognized that in us there dwells no good thing. Without Jesus, we can do nothing. We can't go against Satan with great confidence saying that we can do something, but what we say is "in the name of Jesus, in the authority of that Name (that Name applies a Power-of-Attorney) ... in His Name, we go, and in His Name we have a grant of authority and that is equivalent to a Power-of-Attorney."[3]

One of Satan's favorite weapons is intimidation. He will scheme, threaten, bring fear, and accuse in order to discourage or inhibit us. But we have armor. We have weapons, and we can go boldly on the attack and win the battle against the enemy of the soul. Paul defines the armor we have as Christians and gives us the keys to winning the battle.

> Be strong in the Lord and in his mighty power. Put on the full armor of God so that you can take your stand against the devil's schemes. For our struggle is not against flesh and

blood but against the rulers, against the authorities, against the powers of this dark world and against the spiritual forces of evil in the heavenly realms. Therefore put on the full armor of God, so that when the day of evil comes you may be able to stand your ground, and after you have done everything, to stand. Stand firm then, with the belt of truth buckled around your waist, with the breastplate of righteousness in place, and with your feet fitted with the readiness that comes from the gospel of peace. In addition to all this, take up the shield of faith, with which you can extinguish all the flaming arrows of the evil one. Take the helmet of salvation and the sword of the Spirit, which is the word of God. And pray in the Spirit on all occasions with all kinds of prayers and request. With this in mind, be alert and always keep on praying for all the saints (Eph. 6:10–18).

William Barclay writes,

> The words which Paul uses, powers, authorities, world-rulers, are all names for different classes of these evil spirits. To him the whole universe was a battleground. The Christian had not only to contend with the attacks of men; he had to contend with the attacks of spiritual forces which were fighting against God.... Paul suddenly sees a picture ready-made. All this time he was chained by the wrist to a Roman soldier. Night and day a soldier was there to ensure that he would not escape. Paul was literally an envoy in a chain.... As he writes, the soldier's armor suggests a picture to him. The Christian too has his armor; and part by part Paul takes the armor of the Roman soldier and translates it into Christian terms.[4]

Let us look at the various parts of this armor and the purpose each part serves.

The Belt of Truth

THE BELT OF A Roman soldier served several purposes. The soldier's tunic was tucked into it. The belt, some six to eight inches wide, had to hold tight and be strong enough to carry the weight of a sword and any other weapons needed for hand-to-hand combat. If the belt became loose or fell off in battle, the soldier became vulnerable to the enemy's attack.

Paul likens the soldier's belt to Christian truth. Jesus said, "I am the way and the truth and the life" (John 14:6). Because Christ dwells in believers, the truth is in them. Jesus is the embodiment of truth, and His words are absolute truth.

God has also given us His inspired Word. David said, "How can a young man keep his way pure? By living according to your word" (Ps. 119:9). Jesus prayed, "My prayer is not that you take them out of the world but that you protect them from the evil one" (John 17:15). How are we protected? Jesus said, "Sanctify them by the truth; your word is truth" (v. 17). We must take advantage of God's Word—read it, study it, and apply it in everyday living. As God's Word explains, we must tell the truth and live a life of integrity. We cannot wait until the day of battle; we need to appropriate it today.

When a soldier is suddenly asked to perform on the battlefield, he has already spent much time in preparation for combat. He has disciplined himself to encounter an attack not only defensively—so as to survive—but also offensively—so as to win. So it is with Christians. God the Father has enabled us to come to His Son, Jesus Christ (John 6:44)—at which moment we comprehended eternal truth. Now we must walk in that truth and consistently obey it.

Because the devil understands our weaknesses, he knows exactly what might tempt us to be dishonest. He tries to persuade us to compromise our commitment to telling and living in the truth. Living a life of dishonesty is bondage. When we shun truthfulness, we have to tell one lie after another to cover our tracks.

Paul says that because the first weapon of our armament is to know the truth and to walk in it, we must keep the belt of truth well buckled.

The Breastplate of Righteousness

THE ROMAN SOLDIER'S BREASTPLATE was made of bronze, backed with tough pieces of leather. This protected the soldier's vital organs. A penetrating blow in the front of the torso was likely to be fatal.[5] Our most vulnerable spiritual areas are protected by Christ's imputed righteousness as we serve Him and live for Him.

Someone said, "I can't hear what you are saying because your actions are speaking so loud." After being accused of certain crimes, Plato said, "Well, then, we must live in such a way as to prove that his accusations are a lie."[6] We must demonstrate to a world that is deceived by the father of lies that we can obey the truth and live righteously. God will help us live as we should.

There is an imputed righteousness that we receive because of what Jesus did on the cross. The word *impute* means "to regard or esteem, to consider, to attribute to a person something he does not have, to reckon or credit to one's account." Paul writes, "God made him who had no sin to be sin for us, so that in him we might become the righteousness of God" (2 Cor. 5:21). We cannot earn this righteousness; it is a gift imputed to us through our faith in Jesus Christ. David Wilkerson said,

> If you don't have this truth, the devil will play havoc with your feelings. He'll lie to you and push you around. Unless you have this truth as a foundation under everything you believe, nothing will be right in your doctrine, your theology, your life. You can't even obey God until you understand it![7]

Many Christians are confused and bound by guilt over particular sins. The devil has struck a paralyzing blow with the arm of guilt, shame, and doubt. These believers need only to go to God for forgiveness and cleansing. They cannot "work up" righteous feelings. They must understand that Jesus paid the price for their sins and therefore they are considered righteous. Does this mean that we do not need to be concerned about living righteously? No. When we understand what Christ has done for us, we will have an increased desire to live a life that is holy and pleasing to Him.

The breastplate of righteousness shields us from false pride. It protects us from error. We cannot resist these faults on our own. "Neither can you bear fruit unless you remain in me" (John 15:4). The breastplate also protects us from our insecurities. Nothing "will be able to separate us from the love of God that is in Christ Jesus our Lord" (Rom. 8:39). To "stand our ground"—to stand firm in our righteousness—means to do what is right. If we have to ask our family members to forgive us for being harsh, we do it. If we must apologize to an employee for treating him or her unfairly, we do it. If doing the right thing is more difficult than doing wrong, we always do the right thing anyway. Our righteousness comes from knowing Christ, yet we must progressively walk in righteousness day by day and situation by situation.

The Footwear of Readiness

ANY SOLDIER KNOWS THE importance of having shoes that fit well and have good traction with the ground. A man who has to move quickly or suddenly could fall if the shoes slip.

Sure footing is even more important in our battle with the devil. He knows how to take advantage of any slip that throws us off balance.[8] He will try to divide believers from one another over seemingly insignificant things. He will encourage envy, jealousy, gossip, and disunity in churches. Pastors do well to encourage their congregations to stay focused on the essentials and their reason for being—to win the lost and disciple the found. Some people become more concerned about the color of the wallpaper in the nursery than the fact that their neighbors are dying and going to hell.

The Christian is to wear the right shoes (the gospel) and must always be ready to share the good news with anyone who has not heard it. This good news is a gospel of peace. The world is full of confusion. So many people are lost, disillusioned, and blindly searching for answers in all the wrong places.

Missionary Scott Fontenot met Rene in Vietnam. During the Vietnam war Rene served as a bodyguard to two American diplomats. When a deputy ambassador was injured in a bombing, he insisted that his Vietnamese friend Rene, who was injured trying to protect him, be put in the same hospital room.

Rene tried to bring his family to safety as Saigon fell in 1975, but during the evacuation they got left behind. Within days, Rene was arrested by the North Vietnamese on charges of being an agent of U.S. intelligence. He was severely tortured while serving six years in prison. When he was released, he found that his wife had given up on him.

Shortly afterward, all his children tried to escape from Vietnam on a boat. But their vessel was discovered and sunk in the mouth of a river. Rene and other family members who witnessed the disaster were prevented from rescuing their drowning relatives. Rene was crushed. He had withstood years of torture and the loss of his wife, but as he was forced to watch his children drown, his mind snapped.

Rene attempted to dull the pain in the opium dens that were springing up in his neighborhood. For ten years he was lost in a deep depression and lived in an opium dreamworld. He looked like a madman. His hair was shoulder length, filthy, and matted. His skin was covered with the grime of the streets. His yellow fingernails were so long, they curled back toward his palms. He was uncontrollable, raging at unseen voices that constantly tormented him. To look into his eyes was to look into an abyss of torment, pain, and hatred. He could no longer scrape together the money to smoke opium in the dens.

When Scott and two friends first saw Rene, they knew what they had to do. The three committed Christians began to fast and pray. Two days later, they invited Rene to a church service. During a time of prayer in the service, Rene began to scream and writhe uncontrollably.

The Christians commanded the demons to leave Rene. One by one they left—ten in all. For the first time in several years Rene sat up, in his right mind. "Jesus, save me!" he cried. Tears expressing the joy of sudden freedom streamed from his eyes as he confessed Jesus Christ as his Deliverer, Savior, and Lord.[9]

The gospel of Jesus Christ is truth, it is right, and it will bring peace to the person who understands it. Rene was radically changed. He was given a peace that this world cannot offer, and he was ripped from Satan's dominion by the power of God. Jesus Himself is our peace (Eph. 2:14). Paul shared this message everywhere he went. He didn't let imprisonment stop him from sharing his faith, even with those who were guarding him. He left behind a trail of converts wherever he went. Our feet need to be ready to share this gospel of peace.

The Shield of Faith

THE SHIELDS USED IN the Roman armies were large—about four feet long and two feet wide—in order to protect the soldiers from the most feared weapons of the day. William Barclay writes,

> One of the most dangerous weapons in ancient warfare was the fiery dart. It was a dart tipped with tow dipped in pitch. The pitch-soaked tow was set alight and the dart was thrown. The great oblong shield was made of two sections of wood, glued together. When the shield was presented to the dart, the dart sank into the wood and the flame was put out.[10]

Tow was cloth or twine. The fiery darts were what the New International Version calls "flaming arrows" (Eph. 6:16). Under attack, a soldier could move the shield to the best position and stand behind it, to be protected from these dreadful arrows.

Satan's wicked "flaming arrows" of temptation, opposition, deception, and accusation are penetrating and can incapacitate us. Satan will try to plant a deceptive thought or remind us of something that we have done in the past. He will try to dissuade us from doing what we feel is in the will of God. Our shield of faith is to trust Christ completely and to stay close to Him at all times. Faith is not difficult to understand. We exercise faith in the laws of physics every morning that we get out of bed. We move, put our feet on the ground, and walk away. We subconsciously assume that because this worked yesterday, it will work for us today. We have faith in certain people, imperfect though they be. We have one level of faith or another in a system of government that nevertheless has its flaws.

Our shield of faith is trusting in what Christ has already accomplished for us and applying God's principles to our lives. We can grow in faith by understanding more about God and His Word. "Faith comes from hearing the message, and the message is heard through the word of Christ" (Rom. 10:17). The better we know God's Word and the more we apply it to our lives, the larger shield of faith we will have. We can get struck with this blow or that in the course of life and consequently become disillusioned about our relationship with Christ and what He can do for us. As we grow in faith, our shield can deflect those flaming arrows that the enemy constantly shoots our way.

The Helmet of Salvation

YEARS AGO, MANY STATES passed a law requiring motorcycle riders to wear helmets. The reason was that many motorcycle accidents involved head injuries that led to permanent impairments or death. The laws were intended to provide protection for the head that would spare riders the most severe consequences.

In the same way in spiritual terms, we are to take the helmet of salvation and understand what God has done by offering it to us. God "has qualified you to share in the inheritance of the saints in the kingdom of light" (Col. 1:12). Without Christ we blindly lived in a world of darkness, but now "he has rescued us from the dominion of darkness and brought us into the kingdom of the Son he loves, in whom we have redemption, the forgiveness of sins" (v. 3). He has given us "the right to become children of God" (John 1:12). Our sins have been forgiven and we are cleansed from our sinful acts and thoughts (1 John 1:9). Our helmet of salvation puts us in an entirely different category from those without Christ. Satan knows we are God's children and that he has no rights with us. When he attacks us with temptation or accusation, we can respond and tell him, "I am a child of God, Jesus Christ His son has died for me, and the blood of Jesus covers me. He intercedes for me, and you no longer have any authority in my life." We might not feel this confidence, but by faith we can believe it.

Someone asked Martin Luther, "Do you feel that you have been forgiven?"

He answered,

> No, but I'm as sure as there's a God in heaven. For feelings come and feelings go, and feelings are deceiving; My warrant is the Word of God, naught else is worth believing. Though all my heart should feel condemned for want of some sweet token, there is One greater than my heart whose Word cannot be broken. I'll trust in God's unchanging Word till soul and body sever; For though all things shall pass away, his Word shall stand forever![11]

The Sword of the Spirit

THE SWORD, WHICH IS the Word of God, is the only offensive weapon listed in the armor. Several types of swords were used for battle by Roman soldiers: long, single-edged swords; shorter daggerlike swords; and the *machaira*. The machaira's blade was about two feet long. Both sides had sharp edges, and the blade could quickly penetrate a victim. Soldiers could use this weapon from various positions, swinging it back and forth or thrusting straight on. Most of their enemies used large, single-edged swords that proved awkward against the quickness and agility of the Romans. While the opponent was still positioning himself to swing, he could get stabbed by a machaira.

The Word of God is a double-edged sword (Heb. 4:12). It is powerful against the enemy's attack. It is said that Cromwell's Ironsides regiment fought with a sword in one hand and a Bible in the other.[12] Our spiritual sword can be used in whatever trial or battle the enemy might choose to bring our way. Jesus used the Word to defeat the devil when He was tempted in the wilderness (Matt. 4:1–11).

It is interesting that the biblical writer used the Greek word *rhema* instead of *logos* in Hebrews 4:12. *Logos* refers to proclamation in writing or proclamation as a whole—in our context, to the gospel as a whole. *Rhema,* by contrast, refers to spoken words, with the implication that the speaker is accountable for their intent. The biblical writer has in mind that the "word of God" that we speak to others is a sharp sword. Speaking this word is a powerful weapon when the devil throws his "flaming arrows" at us. We can think the Word, we can read and meditate on the Word, and we can pray the Word. Billy Graham said, "The Bible is the only thing that can combat the devil. Quote the Scriptures and the devil will run.... use the Scriptures like a sword and you'll drive temptation away."[13]

Satan cannot read our thoughts or the intents of our hearts. He watches our conduct and hears what we say. We should let him see that we are dedicated to the Word and let him hear God's eternal, errorless Word expressed in our prayers.

One night I felt a terrible presence of fear in our bedroom. Even though my eyes were closed, I knew there was something at the foot of our bed and, whatever it was, it wanted to bring great harm. I felt paralyzed. I wanted to lie still and pretend that I was asleep, but I knew I needed to make the first move to defend my wife and me. My eyelids felt as if they had heavy weights on them, and when I finally managed to get them open, I saw nothing. Yet I still felt the presence, the fear, and the hatred. Sensing this was a manifestation of the enemy, I thought, "If I can only say the name of Jesus." The words wouldn't come out. Seconds seemed like minutes. Finally I forced the name, "Jesus! Jesus! Jesus!" To my amazement, the presence immediately left. My startled wife said, "What is it? What happened?" I said, "It's okay. Go back to sleep."[14]

Prayer: Our Most Devastating Weapon

D. L. MOODY WROTE in the margin of his Bible, "Prayer must always be the fore-horse of the team. Do whatever is wise, but not till thou hast prayed. Send for the physician if thou art sick, but first pray. Begin, continue, and end everything with prayer."[15]

Our greatest weapon of all—our "heavy artillery"—is prayer. Paul tells us to "pray in the Spirit on all occasions with all kinds of prayers and requests" (Eph. 6:18). We can pray in our own language or in the heavenly language that God has given to many. We can pray in any situation, for anyone, in any location in the world. As the Spirit leads us, we are to be prepared to pray on all occasions. We are to intercede (pray for others), petition (ask for answers to requests), and worship God through prayer. The Lord instructed us to pray for deliverance from the evil one (Matt. 6:13).

Prayer is simply talking to our heavenly Father. He loves us and wants us to communicate to Him our concerns, fears, desires, and weaknesses. As parents, we want our children to know that they can talk to us about whatever concerns them. They can bring their fears to us or express their desires. In response, we can react compassionately and do whatever we can to help them. How much more so will our heavenly Father do such things for us? Prayer is a missile that the devil will never be able to counter with his antiaircraft fire. It is critical that we understand this truth. (See further on this subject in chapter 9.)

Let Us Stand

THE ROMAN SOLDIER HAD some of the best armor that existed and some of the best training. If his armor was fitted correctly, his helmet tightly strapped to his head, his shield in place, and his weapon in hand, there were few foes who could defeat him. When the enemy came, the Roman soldier knew to hold his ground. His training had prepared him to stand and do what he was supposed to do—that is, defeat the one who attacked him. He could stand with confidence, knowing that he had the best equipment and was physically ready for the combat. It is little wonder that the Roman Empire spread far and wide.

There is no doubt that the enemy of our souls will attempt to find times of opportunity to attack us, tempt us, discourage us, accuse us, and thereby defeat us. Evil forces can be found everywhere. "Our struggle is not against flesh and blood, but against the rulers, against the authorities, against the powers of this dark world and against the spiritual forces of evil in the heavenly realms" (Eph. 6:12).

The lion that looks for a weakness so that he can attack is constantly awake. Demon forces are on the search, looking for a habitation like Rene in Vietnam. Satan's powers are strong—make that **strong.** But we must never forget that the armor of God is sufficient enough for us to handle every attack from Satan's kingdom. He might try to tell us that we can't win, but we will triumph if we stand behind the armor. The flaming, wicked arrows can't get through the shield of faith in Christ. Satan cannot penetrate the helmet of salvation, or the breastplate of righteousness in Christ. The sword we wield, God's Word, is sharper and more deadly than any weapon in Satan's arsenal. Our prayers will always help to rout the enemy. With the invincible armor God has provided, we can stand firm and win the spiritual warfare.

Nine ✦

The Arsenal
of Prayer

On Christmas day, the government of Zaire announced that new money had been printed and people had three days to exchange their currency. After December 28 the old money would no longer be recognized. Each person could exchange only three thousand units of the local currency, equivalent to a thousand dollars. This created panic among the people.

Billy could not get to the bank on December 26 because of the crowds and the civil unrest. The next day—Billy and Sue Burr's eighteenth wedding anniversary—Billy was determined to get money exchanged for the mission, so he arrived at the bank at 4:30 A.M. Near the front of the crowd he met six young African men who were also eager to get their money exchanged. With the crowd growing every minute, the seven men agreed to protect each other and their place in line. By ten o'clock there were a great mass of people waiting, but the bank still had not opened. The bank manager decided to open another door, and the stampede began. But in the crush of people, Billy could not move.

Under the hot African sun, some women began to scream that they were dying. No one paid attention, so they started shouting, "The white man is dying!" Billy knew they meant him, since he was taller than most of the Africans and tended to stand out in the crowd.

One of the six men with whom he had made the pact said, "Let him die."

Billy said, "Wait a minute! I thought we were friends. We made an agreement to stick together and see each other through this."

The African replied. "Well, if we Africans all die here today, no one will ever know about our suffering. But if just one American dies, the story will be printed in *Time* or *Newsweek* magazine, and the whole world will know how we suffer."[1]

Sadly, Billy knew that many Africans felt this way, and he became increasingly afraid that he would never get out of the crowd alive.

About two o'clock, a friend saw Billy trapped in the sea of people. The friend hurried to find some soldiers he knew, and he brought them to the edge of the crowd. "Do you see that white man over there?" he asked, pointing to Billy. "He is not here to make money off our people. Please help him."

The soldiers made a human chain and fought their way into the crowd. With a double wristlock they literally dragged Billy out of the crowd. A small Portuguese man who had been standing next to him held onto Billy's clothes, and he was pulled to safety, too. Billy was so weak he could not stand. He was dehydrated and soaked with perspiration. Later, the soldiers escorted him to the bank, and he was able to exchange the funds.

The police used tear gas and fire extinguishers to control the crowd that day. Some in the crowd were blinded by the white powder of the fire extinguishers. Some were killed during the stampede to get inside the banks. Others committed suicide, having lost family fortunes in the monetary changeover.

The situation only became worse over the weeks. People could not get money for food, and Billy wondered. "God, do you know where I am? Do you really know about this situation here?"

One day Kumbali Paul, a former village chieftain who became a dynamic Christian, spoke to Billy. He said, "Two days after Christmas, on December 27, God awakened me very early in the morning. I was startled by a dream I had. In my dream I saw your friends preparing your funeral. I even saw your body in a casket. I was very troubled, so I ran to the church and rang the church bell.

"People came from all over the village to see what the emergency was. They all remembered you from your Christian seminars. I told them about what I had seen and that we had to pray for your safety. We all fell on our knees and began to intercede. After some time, the Lord let me see you up walking around. I told the people that you were going to be fine and thanked them for their prayers."

Billy and Sue were amazed that God encouraged others to pray for them during their crisis. They had heard of this kind of thing happening, but now they experienced it firsthand. Not long after Kumbali Paul spoke to them, they also found out that a woman in Minnesota had been led to pray for them. She wrote, "I have to know what happened to you on December 27! I was awakened very early in the morning with a heavy burden to pray for you. I felt your life was in danger, and I wept and prayed for you. Is there any significance to this burden I felt?"

Billy looked up to toward heaven and said, "Well Lord, you really do know where I am! You know what I'm going through."[2]

Numerous stories can be told of times when God has led people in one country to pray for someone in crisis in another part of the world. Prayer is able to transcend the distance to meet the need and thwart the work of the enemy.

What is prayer? It is conversation with God. It isn't just a rote exercise, learning the prayers at bedtime or from a book of worship. Prayer is much more. It is a wonderful relationship with the Lord wherein we understand that we can call upon Him in the hour of need or temptation or trial. Whatever the problem He will come to our aid. J. Oswald Sanders said, "In prayer, we deal directly with God and only in a secondary sense with men and women. The goal of prayer is the ear of God. Prayer influences men by influencing God to influence them. It is not the prayer that moves men, but the God to whom we pray."[3] Someone else has said, "Prayer moves the arm, that moves the world, to bring deliverance down."[4]

The enemy of the soul knows the power of prayer. It is said that "Satan trembles when he sees the weakest saint on his knees."[5] That is why the devil will encourage us to become too busy to spend time in prayer. Martin Luther said,

I judge that my prayer is more than the devil himself. If it were otherwise I would have fared differently long before this. Yet men will not see and acknowledge the great wonders or miracles God works in my behalf. If I should neglect prayer but a single day, I should lose a great deal of the fire of faith.[6]

Prayer, combined with the Word, helps us build up a resistance so that when Satan assaults us, we instinctively stand our ground because of the sensitivity we have with the Lord. Prayer helps us develop a kind of immune system that gives us the ability to withstand the attacks of the enemy. It isn't something we have to "run to"; it's something that we have in our system. That's why the Bible tells us to be "self-controlled so that you can pray" (1 Peter 4:7); "Pray continually" (1 Thess. 5:17). "Build yourselves up in the most holy faith and pray" (Jude 20).

When believers have not built themselves up through a consistent prayer life, the enemy can attack more freely. Consider a boxer who hasn't trained properly. When he lets down his guard and there is an opening in his defense, his opponent takes advantage of it and knocks him down. When Christians let down their guard, they become subject to the enemy's blows. That's why Scripture tells us that to protect ourselves from the "flaming arrows of the evil one" (Eph. 6:16), we must turn to God in prayer. We draw our strength from the Lord through prayer. When we pray for spiritual strength, for troubled people, or for God's assistance in our lives, we only need to remind ourselves that Jesus said, "Whatever you ask for in prayer, believe that you have received it, and it will be yours" (Mark 11:24). We will only have spiritual strength and the ability to resist the devil according to the quality of our prayer life. Therefore, let's look at the essentials of effective prayer.

Our Supreme Example

WE CAN LEARN MANY things about prayer from Jesus.

- Before He chose the first leaders for the church, Jesus spent the night in prayer (Luke 6:12–13).

- When He was face to face with Satan, Jesus resisted the temptation by using God's Word (Matt. 4).
- When He taught His disciples, Jesus said, "Pray so that you will not fall into temptation" (Matt. 26:41).
- Jesus "went up on a mountainside by himself to pray" (Matt. 14:23).
- On the brink of crises during His ministry, "Jesus often withdrew to lonely places and prayed" (Luke 5:16).
- Jesus consistently showed His disciples that the discipline of prayer is critical for believers (Mark 6:46; Luke 9:28).
- Before He went to the cross, Jesus prayed to bring His will into subjection to the Father's will (Matt. 26:39).

D. M. McIntyre wrote,

> In Luke 5:16 we have a general statement which throws a vivid light on the daily practice of the Lord. "And He withdrew Himself in the deserts and prayed." It is not of one occasion but of many that the evangelist speaks in this place. It was our Lord's habit to seek retirement for prayer. When He withdrew Himself from men, he was accustomed to press far into the uninhabited country—He was in the deserts. The surprise of the onlookers lay in this, that one so mighty, so richly endowed with spiritual power, should find it necessary for Himself to repair to the source of strength, that there He might refresh His weary spirit. To us, the wonder is still greater, that He, the Prince of Life, the Eternal Word, the Only-begotten of the Father, should prostrate Himself in meekness before the throne of God, making entreaty for grace to help in time of need.[7]

We Have Assurance That God Hears

OUR DIVINE CREATOR UNDERSTANDS completely how we are made and knows the strategies of the devil. God has ordained prayer as the way to communicate with Him whether in times of fellowship or times of need.

In a village in southwestern China, the Christian Miao people had made an investment in mulberry trees. The leaves of these trees are used to feed silkworms in the summer. One day in late spring, someone noticed caterpillars eating the mulberry leaves. Soon they were everywhere. Men, women, and even children were sent to pick the caterpillars from the trees. They worked as fast as they could, but their efforts failed to substantially reduce the number of caterpillars. Eventually the workers stopped because pulling the branches was destroying the young leaves.

Pesticides could help, but none were available within a few days' walk, and the Maio did not have the money for such a purchase anyway. The situation looked helpless. "Let's go to church," one believer suggested. "Our efforts are useless. Let us call out to God. Perhaps He will help us."

The other villagers agreed. They made their way across the hill to where the church stood and, with one voice, cried out to God for help. They didn't return to their homes until late that night.

Early the next morning, as one believer aroused himself to return to the chapel, he heard the sound of a crow. Looking into the still, gray sky, he could see a large flock of the blackbirds circling overhead. Suddenly they swept down on the mulberry grove and began feeding on the fat caterpillars.

Miao believers watched from the village as the crows feasted all day. Then, just before evening, the birds retreated over a distant hill, never to be seen again. And in the mulberry grove, not one living caterpillar could be found.[8]

The Miao believers knew what to do when they were out of answers. They cried out to God, and He provided a miracle.

Some people doubt whether God answers every prayer. If God created prayer as the method of communicating with Him, how can we think for a moment that He does not hear us? He may not answer our prayers in the way we would like Him to because He always knows what is best. He sees the whole picture. Even when we think He has not responded, or even heard our pleas,

He could be answering our prayers in His own timing. J. Oswald Sanders writes,

> George Mueller of Bristol prayed for two men for over fifty years that they would become Christians. Someone asked him why he kept on praying for them when there was no obvious response. Mueller replied, "Do you think God would have kept me praying all these years if He did not intend to save them?" Both men became Christians, one just before, one after, Mueller's death.[9]

We must also recognize that God will not answer prayers that are contrary to His divine nature. He will always fulfill His promises according to His character and attributes.

Prayer Protects Us

PRAYER PROVIDES AN IMMUNE system for our spiritual life. It strengthens our resistance to the attacks of the evil one. John Phillips writes,

> The unseen world is a real world, and modern men and women are particularly vulnerable to that spirit world because of their ignorance of it and their inquisitiveness about it. The average person today is like a person living in the Middle Ages, trying to fight disease while ignorant of bacteria. During the plague that decimated London and parts of Britain in 1665, people knew next to nothing about the simplest principles of sanitation. An open city sewer ran down the middle of each street. Rats multiplied. What caused the plague? The Royal College of Surgeons said it was carried by the air. People shut themselves in their houses; stopped up doors, windows, and chimneys. They burned noxious and evil-smelling compounds to battle the enemy, fresh air. Suppose someone had told them that the plague was carried by a bacillus, that the invisible microbes were carried by fleas, and that rats were the chief hosts of the deadly fleas. That person would have been regarded as insane.[10]

There is an evil, invisible force in the world today that is worse than an open sewer or a deadly disease. Satan plagues the human race, seeking to infect it with his poisonous ideas and destructive practices.

Prayer is one of the most potent spiritual antibiotics we have in our fight against this demonic plague. God communicates His will to us through prayer and Bible study. The Holy Spirit who dwells in the believer "intercedes for us with groans that words cannot express" (Rom. 8:26) when we do not know how to pray intelligibly. As we seek to know the will of God for us, the Holy Spirit will encourage us how to pray. He will give us an inner conviction and a sensitivity for how specifically to pray.

The men and women in Scripture who were greatly used of God were people of prayer. E. M. Bounds writes, "They were not leaders because of brilliancy of thought, because they were inexhaustible in resources, because of their magnificent culture or native endowment, but because, by the power of prayer, they could command the power of God."[11]

Through prayer we align ourselves with the Lord, not with the enemy. It is wonderful when a person understands who God is, what He has done, and what He is doing in the world today. It is said that Praying (John) Hyde "prayed as if God were at his elbow."[12] Too many people are ignorant of the devil's devices because they do not spend enough time communing with the Lord.

God knows Satan's ways, and our prayer life can sensitize us to both the enemy's obvious and deceptive strategies. We can become highly trained professionals in the matter of defeating Satan's forces by living a life of discipline and prayer.

Prayer Is Spiritual

OFTEN WHEN WE PRAY we are involved in "spiritual warfare." "Our struggle is . . . against the rulers, against the authorities, against the powers of this dark world and against the spiritual forces of evil in the heavenly realms" (Eph. 6:12).

Regarding this kind of prayer, J. Oswald Sanders writes,

In that phase of the prayer life, three personalities are involved, not two. Between God on the one hand and the devil on the other stands the praying man. Though weak in himself, he occupies a strategic role in the deathless struggle between the dragon and the Lamb. The power and authority he wields are not inherent, but are delegated to him by the victorious Christ to whom he is united by faith. His faith is the reticulating system through which the victory gained on Calvary over Satan and his hosts reaches the captives and delivers them.[13]

Again, think of a Golden Gloves fighter—an amateur—who goes into the ring with a professional boxer. Most people are not professionals. They are novices, observers, and no match for the pro. That professional fighter will find his opponent's weak points in an instant. He is highly skilled in the sport. He has already thought of every angle, every trick, every maneuver that his opponent might use. The knowledgeable professional is ready to respond to the attack of his competitor. The only thing that can beat him is a boxer with equal training who knows his weak points and has the power and strength to defeat him.

This principle holds true for Christians who are trying to fight the devil but pray little. The enemy will hit them with discouragement, despair, fear, apprehension, or temptation and knock them flat on their backs.

D. L. Moody said, "The reason why so many Christians fail all through life is just this—they underestimate the strength of the enemy. My dear friend, you and I have got a terrible enemy to contend with. Don't let Satan deceive you. Unless you are spiritually dead, it means warfare."[14] However, if we have been trained in the discipline of prayer and have prepared ourselves both defensively and offensively, God will give us the strength to overcome the attack even if Satan strikes the first blow—because in Christ we are stronger and more powerful than the enemy. "The one who is in you is greater than the one who is in the world" (1 John 4:4). Prayer is the training circle. It is the training camp for believers in preparation for fighting off the attacks of the enemy so that we can be "more than conquerors" through Him who loves us.

Satan Tries to Keep Us from Praying

SATAN TRIES TO DISHEARTEN us any way he can. The apostle Paul had wonderful victories and made tremendous advances for God's work; he achieved personal successes that few people have known. "God did extraordinary miracles through Paul, so that even hand-kerchiefs and aprons that had touched him were taken to the sick, and their illnesses were cured and the evil spirits left them" (Acts 19:11–12). The believers in Ephesus saw how God used Paul, and they sensed the presence of God in their meetings. They became convicted of behaviors that were not pleasing to God. "Many of those who believed now came and openly confessed their evil deeds. A number who had practiced sorcery brought their scrolls together and burned them publicly" (vv. 18–19).

Yet one day it seemed that the bottom dropped out. Perhaps the people Paul had been ministering to turned against him. Whatever happened, the stress became so overwhelming that Paul did not know if he could go on. His ministry infuriated Satan, who opposed him with all the forces he could assemble. As a result, Paul writes, "We were under great pressure, far beyond our ability to endure, so that we despaired even of life. Indeed, in our hearts we felt the sentence of death" (2 Cor. 1:8–9).

What did Paul do? When he felt that he could not go another step, what was his decision? He turned his attention from his problem to the One who could rescue him. "This happened that we might not rely on ourselves but on God, who raises the dead" (v. 9). Paul might have prayed a prayer similar to this: "Lord, I don't know where to turn, I'm out of ideas, out of strength, and it appears that I'm going to be killed. However, I am going to rely on you. I'm your child, and I trust in you." God delivered Paul from this incredible attack that brought so much despair to his life, because he decided to cry out to God and trust in Him only, and because many were praying for him (v. 11).

David Wilkerson, the founder of Teen Challenge, tells of an experience that could have been very much like that of the apostles.

> Years ago, I was at a large meeting with sister Kathryn Kuhlman in Los Angeles. More than 5,000 people filled the place, with standing room only. At the time, my wife was going through a bout with cancer, and I was carrying the burden of Teen Challenge. I had been traveling and writing, and I'd grown weary and tired. Of course, that's always when the enemy comes to you—when you're physically low, with no strength left.
>
> I was sitting on the stage, waiting to preach, as sister Kuhlman directed the worship. The place was full of God's Spirit, and marvelous things were happening. Yet, suddenly, the enemy came in and whispered to my heart:
>
> "You are the biggest phony on the face of the earth! You're working with troubled people just to make a name for yourself. And now your wife is going to die. You say you've given your life for the Lord's ministry—but it's all vanity! You don't have the fire of God. You've lost your anointing. You can't preach tonight, because all your words will be fake!"
>
> The voice was so loud, I couldn't quiet it. I kept trying to shake it off, but as I stepped up to the pulpit, it was still screaming in my ears. When I opened my mouth to preach, hardly anything came out. I tried for five minutes to speak— but I just couldn't. Finally, I motioned to sister Kuhlman to take over the service, and I turned and walked off the stage.
>
> Backstage a pastor asked me, "David what's wrong? What's the matter?" I could only shake my head. "I'm sorry," I said, "I can't go on. I can't preach tonight. I'm a phony!"[15]

Throughout history Satan has attacked other godly men and women in similar ways. We have known David Wilkerson's ministry—both in Teen Challenge and more recently at Times Square Church—to bring powerful deliverance to those who have become addicted to drugs, alcohol, and hopeless lifestyles. His preaching has literally changed tens of thousands of lives, and he is a wonderful man of God, just the type of person that Satan wants to discourage. The enemy wants to get all of us to a point where we lose the confidence that God hears and answers our prayers.

The devil did not win with Wilkerson, who writes,

In recent years, Satan has tried to play the same "phony" trick on me—but he cannot succeed! Each time I have rebuked him, saying "You broke the record last time, devil. I'll never play that one again. And you'll never convince me I'm a phony!"[16]

The powerful preacher Charles Haddon Spurgeon said, "Prayer pulls the rope below and the great bell rings above in the ears of God. Some scarcely stir the bell, for they pray so languidly; others give but an occasional pluck at the rope. But he who wins with heaven is the man who grasps the rope boldly and pulls continuously, with all his might."[17]

How Should We Pray Against the Enemy?

SOME CHRISTIANS TEACH THAT to be effective in our warfare against the enemy, we need to understand the names of the demons who control "territories"—that is, a country, city, community, or even a whole culture (such as India or Thailand or countries in Africa). Proponents of this theory claim that it is important to identify the evil spirits by name and direct one's prayers specifically against them. Done correctly, those prayers will be effective.

As we mentioned in chapter 3, there is no question that Satan is highly organized and has a detailed strategy to accomplish his goals. His demonic followers are doing his bidding throughout the world. However, Scripture simply does not disclose Satan's strategy or his organizational structures. We believe we should not go beyond Scripture in matters of doctrine. So if God had wanted us to know the names of demons, their territories, and the specific ways to pray against them, He would have given us detailed instructions.

The enemy likes to distract us. Therefore we must be careful not to be so concerned with the devil's strategy and the names of his demons that we miss the perfect plan of God. The Great Commission is for us to evangelize the world with the gospel of Jesus Christ and to make disciples. As the early church was consumed with Jesus Christ, we must be also. With absolute certainty we know that bringing people to Jesus Christ and praying in the name of Jesus will drive away darkness in our communities.

Much misinformation about angels, demons, and spiritual warfare has been disseminated in recent years, often through either fiction or nonfiction books. Frank Peretti is the popular author of *This Present Darkness* and several other fictional books. These books have often been acclaimed as depicting how the enemy works and how to be involved in spiritual warfare. A member of the Assemblies of God denominational staff recently interviewed Peretti for a magazine article. In the interview Peretti touched on some of the reckless teachings currently being bandied about. He emphasized that he never intended to explicate doctrine about spiritual warfare in his writings. Following are some excerpts from the interview.[18]

Editor: Do you consider your books fiction or nonfiction?

Peretti: In terms of an all-sweeping definition I'll say they're fiction, because if I call it nonfiction, then immediately I get into a doctrinal squabble with somebody. I have to be careful to say that this is a creative work of fiction meant to convey a message that inspires. It's not a doctrinal treatise. It isn't an area I want to get too dogmatic in, because I don't know what angels really look like, or how they carry on the warfare. I don't think anybody does.

Editor: What impact do you think your books have had on the Christian world?

Peretti: The most common response is that the book has changed peoples' prayer lives and their awareness of the kind of spiritual warfare that's going on. I almost always hear a comment like, "I knew there was some kind of conflict going on, but I never thought of it as being vivid as you've presented it."

Editor: Were you startled with the success of *This Present Darkness?*

Peretti: I'm still startled by it. People ask me how I explain it and I don't know that I can. I think people are aware that we're all involved in a struggle, and they find something in the book to hang their hat on. I guess I kind of sing everybody's tune. It's what they're feeling, and when they read the book it's something they can relate to. And of course, however God chose to do it, He's touching people's lives and changing their prayer lives through this book.

Editor: What kinds of teachings do you see out there that go over the line?

Peretti: There's a big angel craze going on now. A lot of that is New Age. I think angels are invisible because you're not supposed to be paying attention to them, but worshiping the Lord. Some angels in the Bible say, "Don't worship me. Worship God."

Editor: Have you ever experienced spiritual warfare, or been troubled while working on a book?

Peretti: Not that I know of. I've never had a spooky experience. I have typical stuff like discouragement, depression, and doubt, and I don't even know if demons are responsible. It could have been hormones or something. Everybody goes through his or her own struggles when serving the Lord, and mine are typical as well. A lot of folks ask if Satan attacked me while I was writing these books. I don't think so.

I think the biggest area of struggle was when I was saturated with the subject. It got to be a burden for me, and I became despondent wondering what was going to happen, and wasn't the body of Christ ever going to win? But you know, I just saw the *700 Club* [television program] and they just mentioned what was going on in Pensacola, Florida (a church that is experiencing revival), and I started bawling. "Praise God," I thought. "Here's some good news."

Editor: When you think of the breakdown in the culture of our cities, what gives you hope that the spiritual battle is being won?

Peretti: You have to be careful not to get your kingdoms mixed up. The biggest source of my struggles is when I lament our present culture, but you have to remember that God's covenant is not with the United States of America, it's with His church, and the church of Jesus Christ is actually doing pretty well. Jesus promised He would build it and the gates of hell would not prevail against it. One of these days the church is going to be a beautiful bride without spot or wrinkle, ready for the wedding. You look back through history, and kings and kingdoms have risen and fallen, but the body of Christ has always been here since Jesus started it. It has outlasted every other kingdom and always will. That's where you need to focus your mind and heart. If you look to Washington, D.C., for hope, you're in for a disappointment. Keeping the kingdoms separate is my object.

Editor: Does being well-known frustrate you as a writer or in your walk with Christ?

Peretti: It doesn't frustrate me in my walk with Christ. I attend my own little church and do the usual church thing. I have a pastor and brothers and sisters in the Lord. I'm involved in the worship team and just do normal Christian things, which are real important. When I go out, I seem to be this giant—which I'm not, but I'm made to look that way. I find that intimidating. I'm supposed to know all about this stuff, and I don't. People ask tough questions and expect a lot more of me than I'm equal to.

Prayer in the name of Jesus is sufficient. It is enough. We must not complicate the issue of spiritual warfare. Every Christian believer is able to win. God sees clearly the young and the old, the new Christian and the mature Christian, those who are highly intelligent and those who are not as gifted, people of any culture or color or language or people group who have lived at any time. We do not. God tells us that the person who lives an obedient life and consistently prays will win the battle.

In his book *Storm Warning*, Billy Graham writes about a direct confrontation with the enemy in two of his crusades.

> One night in Nuremberg, Germany, we were holding a crusade in the same stadium in which Hitler used to stage his infamous rallies. It was difficult to sit in that place and hear in the echoes of memory the masses shouting "Sieg, Heil!" ... Then one night, as I sat on the platform, Satan worshipers

dressed in black assembled just outside the stadium doors. Using ancient, evil rites, they tried to put a hex on the meeting. The rumor of their presence spread, Christians prayed, and in answer to those prayers, nothing came of the incident.

Another night in Chicago, three hundred Satan worshipers approached McCormick Place with the specific intent of taking over the platform and stopping the crusade service that was in progress. They announced their plan in advance, but I didn't dream they would actually try to storm the platform. We had just sung the second hymn of the evening. George Beverly Shea had sung a gospel song, and Cliff Barrows was about to lead a massed choir in a great anthem of praise. At that moment a policeman rushed to the stage and whispered something to the mayor, who was present that night to welcome us.

At the same moment, the Satan worshipers forced their way past the ushers at the rear of that spacious auditorium and were proceeding down the back aisles toward the platform. There were more than thirty thousand young people in our Youth Night service. Only those seated near the back saw the Satan worshipers enter. The mayor of Chicago turned to me and said, "Dr. Graham, we'll let the police handle these intruders."

"Let me try it another way, Mr. Mayor," I suggested. I then interrupted the choir's song and addressed the thirty thousand young people there in McCormick Place. I explained, "There are about three hundred Satan worshipers now entering the auditorium. They say they're going to take over the platform. You can hear them coming now."

The crowd could hear the rising chant of the Satan worshipers. Everyone turned to see them moving with determination down the aisles, past the ushers who were working to restrain them. They were causing a considerable disturbance by that time. I continued addressing the crowd. "I'm going to ask you Christian young people to surround these Satan worshipers," I exhorted. "Love them. Pray for them. Sing to them. And gradually ease them back toward the entrances through which they have come."

I will never forget that moment! Hundreds of young Christians stood to their feet and did exactly as I had asked. Some grabbed hands and began to sing. Others put their arms around the Satan worshipers and began to pray for them. Others calmly shared their faith with them. Everyone else at McCormick Place sat praying as God's Spirit moved through His people to confound the work of Satan in our midst. I stood watching in silence. I waited and prayed until peace was restored and the service could resume.[19]

Billy Graham, the people of Nuremberg, and these youth in Chicago saw firsthand how the power of prayer and a demonstration of the love of God can force the enemy back.

How can we consistently pray in ways that will defeat the enemy? God wants us to understand that we are all able to succeed in prayer and to resist the enemy. Several principles are unfolded consistently throughout the pages of Scripture:

1. We should understand that we are not in a conflict in the physical realm of flesh and blood but with spiritual forces and powers of evil (Eph. 6:12). Prayer is spiritual, and there is a spiritual world around us that constantly tries to induce us to compromise our faith or become discouraged. Reading, studying the Bible, and praying will keep us on the winning side when the spiritual forces that are against God attempt to throw us off track.

Years ago, I asked the Lord to put me on a schedule of rising early in the morning so I could read my Bible and pray. Since my college days I have had a devotional life, but I wanted to spend more time with the Lord every day. God answered my prayer, and it seemed that I naturally started waking up around 5:00 A.M. Since that day, my habit is to go to my study and read my Bible, study the Word, pray about what I have read, and pray through my prayer list. Even though my schedule, like most people's, seems very full, this two-hour devotional time is the most important appointment of my day.

I spend this time with the Author of Life—the One who knows me better than I know myself and the One who understands every person and situation I will face during the day. He can keep me calm when in my flesh I would become nervous. He can give me peace when a situation would normally bring great concern. He can give me the words to say when my natural intellect isn't sufficient. He knows the tricks of the devil and will be my rearguard against the enemy's attempts to deceive, distort, or distract.[20]

Our prayer life is critical. Through it God will help us to be sensitive to the principalities and powers that would injure us and those we love.

2. We should pray that we will live a life before God, fervently committed to His truth and righteousness (Rom. 12:1–2; Eph. 6:14). Every day we need to die to our flesh and decide to live for God in everything we do and say. Paul said that "I die every day" (1 Cor. 15:31). We shouldn't worry about tomorrow, next week, or next year. If we live one day at a time, we will develop godly habits that will help us be victorious over the enemy or the challenges of life tomorrow.

3. We should pray in faith, knowing that Satan's power can be broken in any specific area of his domain (Acts 26:18; Eph. 6:16; 1 Thess. 5:8). In Christ we can do all things. There is no habit, addiction, or wrong lifestyle that with God's help we cannot overcome. There is no painful experience from which we cannot receive God's supernatural healing. With God's help we can forgive anyone who has hurt us and thereby become free from that injury. Even when we do not feel free, we can pray by faith and God will help us, either supernaturally or through a godly friend. Jesus came to give us an abundant life.

4. We should realize that as believers in Jesus Christ we have been given powerful spiritual weapons for the destruction of Satan's strongholds (2 Cor. 10:4). Our prayer life is one of those powerful weapons. When we pray, the enemy cowers. When we pray, we are communicating with the Creator God, our Heavenly Father, who loves us and will respond to our prayers.

5. We should pray that God will give us daily opportunities to share the gospel with someone. There is tremendous spiritual victory when we proclaim the Gospel of the Kingdom in the power of the Holy Spirit (Matt. 4:23; Luke 1:15–17; Acts 1:8; 2:4; 8:12; Rom. 1:16; Eph. 6:15). When we witness, give our Christian tes-

timony, or teach about Jesus Christ, spiritual seeds are planted that the Holy Spirit will cause to grow in that other person's life. In doing this we are directly challenging the enemy that would like to keep people blind to the truth.

6. We should challenge Satan and his power directly by praying in Jesus' name (Acts 16:16–18), by using the Word of God (Eph. 6:17), by praying in the Spirit (Acts 6:14; Eph. 6:18), by fasting (Matt. 6:16; Mark 9:29), by casting out demons (Matt. 10:1; 12:28; 17:17–21; Mark 16:17; Luke 10:17; Acts 5:16; 8:7; 16:18; 19:12). These activities are to be normal for the Christian, just as they were in the early church. This is aggressive praying and aggressive living.

7. We should pray that the Holy Spirit will produce conviction in the lost in regard to sin, righteousness, and the coming judgment (John 16:7–11). Often God will bring people to us who are struggling with a lifestyle or lack peace, and we should view these occasions as opportunities offered by the Holy Spirit for us to give godly counsel, pray for them, introduce them to Christ, or give scriptural guidance.

8. We should pray that we will be used of God in the supernatural gifts (Acts 4:29–33; 10:38; 1 Cor. 12:7–11). There is no question that the early church experienced signs and wonders. We believe that we will see God move in similar ways in our day.[21]

There is a renewed prayer movement going on around the world today. It seems that the Christian church has come alive with the passion to pray. In our book *Back to the Word*, we write,

> The evangelical scholar J. Edwin Orr summarized, into one statement, his sixty years of historical study on great prayer movements preceding spiritual awakenings. He says, "Whenever God is ready to do something new with his people, he always sets them to praying." If this is true and foundational to God's agenda, when revival is on the horizon, then a worldwide revival is coming. The most hopeful sign of our times is the prayer movement.
>
> David Barrett, a noted demographer of the Christian movement in the world today, has gathered the following statistics:

1. Worldwide there are about 170 million Christians who are committed to praying daily for world evangelization and spiritual awakening (revival).

2. Of this group, twenty million believe that praying for world revival is the primary calling that God has given them. They are what we call "prayer warriors."

3. Around the world are at least ten million prayer groups that have a common focus in prayer each time they meet. They continually ask God to bring worldwide revival.

4. Worldwide there are an estimated thirteen hundred prayer mobilization networks endeavoring to persuade the church to pray more for world revival.

David Bryant, an evangelical prayer movement leader, commented on this modern-day phenomenon respecting prayer: "If we know historically, as Dr. Orr suggests, this groundswell of prayer is a gift of God; if it is biblically accurate to teach that God has not only ordained the end but also the means (the end being world revival, the means being the prayers of his people); if this massive chorus of prayer is increasingly focused on nothing less than national and world revival; and if, when God stirs us up to this type of praying he does so because he is actually ready to answer us—how can we believe otherwise than that world revival is bearing down on top of us."[22]

The renewal and revival that all kinds of people are experiencing is a result of prayer. This revival in not within one denomination or fellowship. It is a revival that ranges across the body of Christ to pray, worship, and win this world for God's kingdom.

PART THREE

OUR ULTIMATE VICTORY

Ten

Satan's Present-day Strategies

The Red Cross supervisor for the region of Ogaline, Croatia, was eager to meet with an American who had studied psychology and human behavior. His assignment was to help the refugees in his sector as much as possible with the resources available to the Red Cross. He had witnessed the bombing of the hospital in his community the week before. Fighting was going on all around him, and he wondered whether his refugee camps might be bombed next.

The supervisor, whom we'll call John, felt great compassion for the many women and children in desperate need. Daily he heard their pleas for help in finding their husbands and fathers, some of whom had been missing for up to two years. He really had no way of knowing these men's whereabouts, but feared that if they had not been heard from in several months, they were probably dead or, at best, in a prisoner-of-war camp. All he could offer these families was words of hope, but inside he had little hope himself.

When I arrived,[1] John quickly assembled his leadership team around the large oak table in the dimly lit room. He asked his assistant to bring some cookies and coffee. He apologized to me that he didn't have more to offer, then hurriedly got to his point: "I am wondering if you could offer me some advice about how to help the children in the refugee camps. A high percentage of them are suffering depression, and some are exhibiting some behavior that is not normal."

The Red Cross workers with him added, "Many of the children have not seen or heard from their fathers for several months and some, for over a year. Their mothers are depressed, too. They have lost their homes and all of their belongings other than what they could carry to the camp. They seem to be in shock."

"Do you have any type of educational program going on?" I asked. "Are there activities that the children can become involved in every day? What do the women in the camps do every day?"

John responded, "We do not have the books or materials to provide any educational assistance to the children, and we have very little activities for the women. Our resources are limited."

After more than an hour of discussion, I offered to get some curriculum and writing materials to John within the next few weeks for a school program for the children. I encouraged him to start some kind of activities for the women that would help them pass the time. He was grateful.

The sun was going down, and John warned, "I need to get you to the refugee camp soon, as you shouldn't drive in this area after dark."

We drove past military personnel and equipment—buildings that had been bombed within the last few days—and as we approached the refugee camp, I felt concerned that I might be there if someone decided to attack the camp. Then I thought ashamedly, *These people have these kinds of concerns every day. At least I can leave the country in a few days—they can't.*

As I lay in the bed provided for me, I wondered, *Why are these innocent people suffering so much? Why is this war going on?* I was half-awake most of the night to listen for any nearby bombing.

In the morning, hundreds of women and children gathered in a makeshift auditorium after breakfast to listen to the Christian music group that was traveling with me. We passed out candy and some small gifts, sang Christian songs, and then talked to them about the love of God and His concern for them. As I spoke, I saw tears falling from mother's faces and children beginning to smile, and for a brief moment in their lives, I saw some hope. I thought, *This moment is worth the trip.*

At the conclusion of the message I gave an invitation to come to Christ. The front of the room became full of people who wanted to become Christians. I was overwhelmed with their response. Over and over again, I heard the comment, "Thank you for coming. Can you come back again?" Others said, "This is a wonderful gift you have given us. We haven't had this much joy since we have been here."

In a few hours we were driving through northern Croatia to visit another refugee camp. My heart was heavy with concern for the children that I had bonded with. I wondered about their future. How many of them would never see their fathers again? I fought back the tears. I pondered what Jesus had said about the last days: "You will hear of wars and rumors of wars, but see to it that you are not alarmed. Such things must happen, but the end is still to come. Nation will rise against nation, and kingdom against kingdom" (Matt. 24:6–7). The thought didn't elevate the sorrow I felt for those innocent refugees, but it did remind me that we are very possibly in those final days that Jesus warned us about, when Satan will increase his activity as never before. The women and children in Ogaline were suffering because the enemy does not care whom he hurts in trying to distract people from a loving God.

The Battle Has Intensified

SCRIPTURE TELLS US THAT in the last days wickedness will increase and demonic influence will become more evident. "The Spirit clearly says that in later times some will abandon the faith and follow deceiving spirits and things taught by demons" (1 Tim. 4:1). "But mark this: There will be terrible times in the last days" (2 Tim. 3:1).

Jesus Christ warned that there would be an outbreak of satanic counterfeit miracles in the epoch of time preceding His return. "For false Christ's and false prophets will appear and perform great

signs and miracles to deceive even the elect—if that were possible. See, I have told you ahead of time" (Matt. 24:24–25).

Similarly, Paul writes, "The coming of the lawless one will be
in accordance with the work of Satan displayed in all kinds of
counterfeit miracles, signs and wonders, and in every sort of evil
that deceives those who are perishing. They perish because they
refused to love the truth and so be saved" (2 Thess. 2:9–10).

Never in human history have the evil events of the end time,
as described in the Bible, been more in evidence than they are
now. In this day of technology it seems that Satan is accelerating
and intensifying his strategy to control the world.

Gen. Matthew B. Ridgway, former U.S. Army Chief of Staff,
wrote in his autobiography, *Soldier*, "There are two kinds of information that no commander can do without—information per-
taining to the enemy which we call 'combat intelligence' and
information on the terrain. Both are vital."[2]

It is critical in wartime to discern where the enemy will attack.
Accurate, pertinent, and timely intelligence on the enemy is neces-
sary for making an adequate defense. It is fundamental to have sure
knowledge of the strength of the enemy. What is his plan of attack?
What is his timing? What is his next move? What weapons will he
likely use? This information is needed if we would win battle.

Scripture offers much prophetic information as to how Satan
will attempt to influence and control the terminal generation before
the second coming of Jesus Christ. We could be that last generation.

Satan is not stupid. We need to assume that he knows our
weak points and where to target us with his temptations. Where
one person might be strong, another will be weak. The devil's
modus operandi is different with every person. This generation
has seen occult practices spread worldwide, through television
programs, New Age teaching, alleged abductions by unidentified
flying objects (UFOs), witchcraft, and psychic phone lines.

New cults and false religions emerge and grow rapidly,
because Satan seeks to divert people from the Truth.

For many, human life is demeaned through legalized abortion
that results in about one and a half million babies being killed each

year. Arguments rage over the "quality of life" and the morality of euthanasia and physician-assisted suicide. It is reported that a new computer program, used in the first legally assisted death in Australia, will soon be available on the internet. Philip Nitschke, a doctor and the author of the book *Self-Deliverance,* states that the program is only a small part of a death package that includes a machine for delivering lethal injections.[3]

We should realize that this hideous crime of euthanasia will only escalate. Its victims will extend from the terminally ill, to the depressed, the physically weak, the person with a death wish, the elderly, and perhaps anyone who a particular group of people feel are not contributors to society. It is a frightening thought! If the Nazi party could convince their people of a right to exterminate certain kinds of people because of their religious beliefs or ethnic culture or physical condition, we should assume that this type of ethnic cleansing and murder can be repeated. History often repeats itself. The enemy of our souls would like us to think that after physical, conscious life ends, there is nothingness. This devastating lie has persuaded countless people to end their lives prematurely or to take someone else's life unnaturally.

In her book *Power, Pathology, Paradox: The Dynamics of Good and Evil,* Marguerite Shuster insightfully comments,

> The Fallen Angel would say that there is no heaven, no other hope, and therefore no hell; the Prince of the world would say that there is no other world, and therefore no God or Satan; the Tempter, that there is no judge, and hence no offense or Author of Evil; the Liar, that there is no reality, thus no lie or Liar; Legion, that there is no person so he cannot exist; and the Accuser, that there is no pardon.[4]

There is no question that evil has escalated in our generation and that the enemy has heightened his attack on mankind in myriad ways as he prepares for the final battle. Shuster accurately portrays a part of Satan's strategy to deceive people:

> To characterize the Devil as essentially "anti" is to say that his intent and procedure is to isolate, to deceive, and to

destroy; to break down the integrity of relationships and of mind and body—it matters little which comes first, as any one of them can easily bring the others in its train. If he is finally to succeed, however, he cannot remain a force wholly external to persons but, as we have seen, must snare them as willing followers. Thus we must see his "anti" stance as extending even to his own appearance: he masquerades as good, as an angel of light (2 Cor. 11:14). His very nature is to lie: "He is a liar and the father of lies" (John 8:44; the Greek implies him to be the father of his own lies, such that even a standard of truth is denied, which is the most absolute lie possible). He wishes to persuade us that all is relative, that contraries are indifferent, that white is really gray is really black. He would represent things to us as he chooses; he would make all appearances lie and make faith itself heretical and godless (1 Tim. 4:1). To take him seriously is to expect him where we do not expect him. From his subtlety in the Garden to his signs and lying wonders in the Apocalypse, he presents evil as good. He counterfeits God. Thus human "goodness" or innocence cannot itself prevail.[5]

Signs of the Last Days

THE BIBLE GIVES MANY details about the last days, when Satan will subtly attempt to keep as many people in his kingdom as possible. There are many false gods extant in the world.

Humanism is a common religion in the world. Humanism is the worship of self instead of God. People will be interested in their own welfare, values, and interests without taking God into consideration. In their selfishness to satisfy their desires, they will forget God and worship the creature rather than the Creator (Rom. 1:22–23, 25; 2 Tim. 3:2). Even more pernicious than this egocentric way of living are religions that teach that people can actually become gods. This false concept is common in New Age teaching. Also, Mormonism teaches, "As man is, God once was, and as God is, man may become." The founder of the Mormon church said, "God was once a man like us and dwelt on an earth, the same as Jesus Christ did, and you have got to learn to be gods yourselves the same as all gods before you."[6]

The spirit of humanism began with the prideful Lucifer. He thought only of himself, and this lurid thought turned into the idea that he could be as powerful as God. Satan himself has promoted self-centered humanism.

Materialism is a common false god. People want more and more material belongings and money. Greed will increase world-wide (Rom. 1:29).

Not long after the Iron Curtain came down in Eastern Europe, I had the opportunity to visit many Christian leaders in Timisoara, Romania. I found the churches in that country full of faith, power, and a deep love for God. Yet, the people were poor and had few material possessions. They couldn't be sure they would have enough food to get their families through another winter. Most of their clothing was worn, old, and tattered—but clean. What few automobiles could be seen on the roads were usually old and plain. I thought, *These people have suffered for over thirty years, and have so few earthly possessions—yet they are full of faith in God, have a deep love for one another, and are happy.* I concluded that the church in Eastern Europe has become stronger in spite of their great persecution and lack of material blessings.

I asked a leading pastor from Timisoara what he felt was the greatest threat to the church of Romania now that the walls of tyranny had fallen. Without hesitation, he said, "Teachings that say you only have to name it, and claim it, then you will have it. When people start looking to material things to obtain happiness, rather than to their God, then their faith will begin to decrease."

I had to agree with him. Because of their lack, they wholly depended on God to supply their every need. Day by day, hour by hour, moment by moment, they trusted the One who would care for them.

Satan wants us to think that our happiness, peace, content-ment, and feelings of security come from what we own. In the last days this lie will deceive many into looking to material gain as the mark of success. There is no question that God often blesses His people materially and will supply their needs. But our joy and peace come from the Lord and not from what we own. All over the world there are dynamic, committed believers in Jesus Christ who have very little in earthly possessions, but give a wonderful demonstration of the blessing of God on their lives.

Hedonism is a common lifestyle. The devotion to pleasure and self-gratification, accompanied by a disregard for conventional morality, is rapidly becoming a way of life. The achievement of pleasure, no matter what the cost, is the goal of many today. The Bible states that people will be lovers of self more than lovers of God or His will (2 Tim. 3:2–4). People will try to suppress the truth about God (Rom. 1:18–22, 30). Many would like to put an end to God's Word and His truth. People will give themselves over to sexual impurity (Rom. 1:24) and become more open about homosexual behavior (vv. 26–27).

Television, movies, videos, gimmicks, and games continually promote a hedonistic attitude. They try to communicate that Christian values and principles are old-fashioned. Their message, whether promoting immorality or denigrating religious faith, becomes bolder and bolder as we approach the end of the age.

Nihilism—despair—is a common condition. As people alienate themselves from a holy God, love will grow cold (Matt. 24:12). People will become more and more out of control because of their abuse of morality (Rom. 1:28–32). When people ignore God and His will, difficult times come (2 Tim. 3:2–4). There will be more and more violence and lawlessness. People will become more arrogant and even brag about their ungodly behavior. Mocking God and even blaspheming Him will be common (see Rom. 1:30; 2 Tim. 3:2–4). Paul warned Timothy that these days would be difficult (2 Tim. 3:1).

Many will suffer because of this rejection of God's principles. There will be a rebellious spirit among children (2 Tim. 3:2), maliciousness (gossip, slander, envy, malice, vv. 2–4), deceit (Rom. 1:29, 31), betrayal by family members (Mark 13:12), stress to the point that "men will faint from terror" (Luke 21:26), and people will hate good (Rom. 1:29; 2 Tim. 2:3). The day will be full of despair.

More specifically, as we move into a new millennium, there are major fronts that the enemy has in focus. These include marriage, church unity and church attendance, evangelism, prayer, morality, and God's Word.

The Attack on Marriage

THERE IS A DEMON-INSPIRED attack on the divine institution of marriage and on individual marriages. Among Paul's warnings about the doctrines that deceiving spirits will promote is the curious idea of "forbidding to marry" (1 Tim. 4:3 KJV). Although it is impossible to say to how much demonic influence is affecting the institution of marriage today, it is obvious that marriage is different from what God created it to be.

This attack on marriage has even affected the Christian community. The Barna Research Group made the following report based on interviews with 3,142 randomly selected adults in the United States, including 1,220 born-again Christians.[7]

- Consistent with our earlier findings, we discovered that one out of every four adults (24 percent) who has been married has experienced a divorce.[8]
- Born-again Christians are slightly *more* likely than non-Christians to go through a divorce. Twenty-seven percent of Christians have seen their marriage break up, compared with 23 percent of non-Christians.
- Adults who describe themselves as Christian fundamentalists are more likely than others to get divorced: 30 percent have experienced divorce.
- Data comparing the ages at which people were married and at which they accepted Christ as their Savior show that accepting Christ does not reduce the incidence of divorce. Eighty-seven percent of adult Christians who said they had been divorced at one time or another got divorced while they were Christians.

Satan seeks to destroy marriages, not only for the havoc divorce wreaks on adults and children, but for the discredit divorce brings on Christianity.

G. H. Pember speaks of some of the demonic doctrines about marriage prevailing today.

> Spiritualists of the school with which we have now to deal teach that the marriage of male and female is the great institution of the next life and that every person has an affinity who will be his or her spouse for eternity, but that in this present time there were frequent mistakes, and that consequently those who are not spiritual affinities being joined together are unable to agree and live in union. This they affirm to be the cause of all misfortune in wedded life.

> Many Spiritualists, however, go much further, and declare that marriage should last only so long as the contracting parties may be disposed to live together, in short that God's first ordinance, like every other restraint, is to be snapped asunder as soon as it becomes wearisome.[9]

Prime-time television constantly challenges traditional marriage, even mocking the idea that marriage is to last a lifetime. Don Wildmon reports that 88 percent of sexual activity in prime-time television is between people who are not married, thus making "lust more attractive than love."[10]

Many of the daily talk shows seem to exalt sexual perversion. For example, one of the guests on a recent daytime talk show was a woman who claimed to have had sex with 250 men in the span of ten hours.[11]

Wildmon wrote about the moral content of one calendar quarter in television.

> The fall season, with the exception of Christmas specials, saw the continuance of network television's "politically correct" (PC) programming in almost every imaginable area—the denigration of religion, particularly the Christian faith; the advocacy of homosexuality, mercy killing, promiscuity and teen sex; and the redefining of the concept of family to diminish traditional ideas.[12]

It should be no wonder to us that television programmers promote so much of the activity that disgusts those in the Christian faith. Linda and S. Robert Lichter of the Center for Media and Public Affairs in Washington, D.C., along with Stanley Rothman of Smith College have written a well-documented report on the "media elite." They did an important survey of 104 of the "most influential television writers, producers, and executives."[13] Following are some of their findings:

- Ninety-three percent "say they seldom or never attend religious services."
- Ninety-seven percent "believe that a woman has the right to decide for herself whether to have an abortion."
- Eighty percent "do not regard homosexual relations as wrong."
- Only 5 percent "agree strongly that homosexuality is wrong," compared with 49 percent who "disagree strongly."
- Eighty-six percent "support the rights of homosexuals to teach in public schools."
- Fifty-one percent "do not regard adultery as wrong."
- Only 17 percent "strongly agree that extramarital affairs are wrong."[14]

It can no longer be assumed that when a man and a woman become married, they are making a lifetime commitment. More and more people are allowing for the possibility that "if this one doesn't work out, I'll just get out of the marriage and find someone else."

Premarital sex appears to be a norm in our society. A majority of people who marry this year will have cohabited with someone already, even though statistics show that cohabitation greatly increases the likelihood of divorce.[15]

Extramarital affairs are on the increase. One-third of Americans believe it is acceptable for two people to have an affair as long as both of them want the affair to happen.[16]

Several states are considering legalizing marriages between two people of the same sex. In some places in America, homosexual couples are permitted to adopt children.

When we look at what has happened to the family in our generation, we should not doubt that Satan has declared war on the home. Why? Because the home that operates according to godly principles is the second greatest institution on earth, second only to the church.

The Attack on Morality

LARRY POLAND WRITES IN a newsletter of the battle being waged by Hollywood film, video, and television producers to influence the minds of anyone who watches their creations:

> Seventy-five years of films, fifty years of TV, and decades of recorded music have evidenced increasing control from the "dark side." Occult images fill even children's films, cartoons, and video games.
>
> Music videos have turned increasingly pornographic and rap musicians spew forth obscenities and blasphemies.
>
> More than fifty "black metal" and "death metal" rock/rap groups preach satanic messages and even call for the worship of the Prince of Darkness.[17]

In his weekly pastor's briefing, H. B. London of Focus on the Family reported, "The third most popular album in America this week is Marilyn Manson's 'Antichrist Superstar,' featuring the following messages for teens: 'I will bury your God in my warm spit' and 'Let's just kill everyone and let your God sort them out.'"[18]

This kind of hideous, degrading, blasphemous verbiage leaves no doubt that the enemy is targeting our young people's morals and Christian beliefs through popular music, MTV, telvision programming, movies, videos, and online services.[19] Even the popular Disney corporation, which for years has promoted clean family entertainment, has compromised its positive message. An upcoming Disney album, titled "Blackacidevil," by the extremely satanic rock group, Danzig, was released the day before Halloween 1996. *Growing Up Gay,* a book for teenagers published by Disney-owned Hyperion Press, encourages readers to explore the homosexual lifestyle. Disney's acquisition of Miramax and the subsequent production of the movie *Priest,* a film about a homosexual cleric, demonstrate that this organization has changed from its positive family message. An annual Gay and Lesbian Day celebration has been held at Disney World for several years as families innocently visited the park seeking wholesome entertainment.

Roseanne Arnold, star of the popular TV situation comedy *Roseanne,* has commented about pro-life proponents, many of whom are Christians, this way:

> You know who else I can't stand is them [sic] people that are anti-abortion. [Expletive deleted] them, I hate them. . . . They're horrible, they're hideous people. They're ugly, old, geeky, hideous men. . . . They just don't want nobody [sic] to have an abortion 'cause they want you to keep spitting out kids so they can [expletive deleted] molest them.[20]

Before a typical American child finishes elementary school, he or she will have seen an average of eight thousand murders and one hundred thousand acts of violence portrayed on television.[21]

George Barna said, "America is headed for either anarchy or revival in five to ten years. . . . The church has not prevented a massive moral and ethical decline in America." Barna cites these statistics: "A majority of people who marry this year will have cohabited with someone before getting married; one-third of Americans believe it is acceptable to two people to have and affair with each other; and half of the people marrying this year believe they will divorce. Also, 71% of American adults believe there is no such thing as absolute truth, a view shared by 64% of born-again Christians and 40% of evangelical Christians."[22]

Barna adds, "Ninety-six percent of American adults believe in God, but 45 percent believe Jesus committed sins while on earth. A majority of Americans believe salvation may be found in either of two ways: through relation with Jesus Christ or through good works. Americans aren't keeping the 10 Commandments because they don't know them; 58 percent of American adults cannot name half of the commandments."[23]

This attack on godly morals is hardly surprising, because Satan promotes darkness and evil behavior while God is a God of light and holiness.

> But you, brothers, are not in darkness so that this day should surprise you like a thief. You are all sons of the light and sons of the day. We do not belong to the night or to the darkness. So then, let us not be like others, who are asleep, but let us be alert and self-controlled. For those who sleep, sleep at night, and those who get drunk, get drunk at night. But since we belong to the day, let us be self-controlled, putting on faith and love as a breastplate, and the hope of salvation as a helmet. For God did not appoint us to suffer wrath but to receive salvation through our Lord Jesus Christ (1 Thess. 5:4–9).

The Attack on Evangelism

CONCURRENT WITH THE CULTURAL assault on morality, this day in the life of the church has become a great period of evangelism, which constitutes a powerful threat to Satan's kingdom.

Ralph Reed, executive director of the Christian Coalition, writes, "How will our times be viewed by history? I believe these days will be remembered as a time of remarkable spiritual awakening. The greatest revival of religion in modern times is breaking across the globe."[24]

Bill Bright, president of Campus Crusade for Christ, says, "Lately I have sensed that the body of Christ is on the verge of the greatest spiritual breakthrough in the history of Christianity."[25]

D. James Kennedy, the founder and president of Evangelism Explosion, comments that when

> Peter preached his first sermon there were three-thousand who believed. Shortly thereafter, five thousand more were added to the number, followed by a great multitude of Jews and priests! Next came a time of persecution, and when it ended in A.D. 313 with the Edict of Toleration, there were

about ten million professing Christians alive. By the year 1000, this number had grown to fifty million. By the end of the 1700s, most of the missionary impetus had stalled, yet the number had grown to 215 million professing Christians. That is an increase of 165 million in eight hundred years.

In 1795 the modern missionary movement began in earnest with William Carey. By the year 1900, the number had grown to five hundred million professing Christians. That is an increase of 285 million in one century. And then by 1980, just eighty short years later, that number had grown to 1.3 billion professing Christians. Then by 1990, that number had grown to roughly 1.8 billion—an increase of 1.3 billion people in the twentieth century alone! There is nothing even vaguely approaching this accomplishment in the annals of human history.[26]

Remember that these numbers include all professing believers in every Christian denomination—Protestant, Catholic, and Orthodox. But even though how many of these are evangelical, "Bible-believing Christians" is unknown, their number grows larger every day.

David Barrett, a church demographer, compared the estimated number of evangelical Christians with the number of non-Christian people in the world at different points in history:

One to ninety-nine by 1430
One to forty-nine by 1790
One to thirty-two by 1940
One to twenty-four by 1960
One to nineteen by 1970
One to sixteen by 1980
One to thirteen by 1983
One to eleven by 1986
One to ten by 1989
One to nine by 1993[27]

Barrett further states, "The Kingdom of Christ is expanding even faster, at over three times the rate of world population."[28]

Most of this church growth is occurring outside the United States, though there are signs of a new growth trend in America. One church in Pensacola, Florida, has seen more than 60,000 decisions for Christ in just over eighteen months. A church in Urbana, Illinois, has had more than 500 converts in just a few months. The pastor of a church in Grand Rapids, Michigan, that had been experiencing much growth felt that God wanted him to begin a prayer meeting on Friday nights. The pastor wondered whether anyone would come to church on a Friday night, but now more than 2,000 people turn out week after week.

A unique stirring has been going on throughout America on public and Christian college campuses, in men's and women's groups, among the youth, and in churches of many denominations. It seems that God is "pouring out His Spirit" like no other time in history.

The prophet Joel writes,

"I will pour out my Spirit on all people.
Your sons and daughters will prophesy,
   your old men will dream dreams,
   your young men will see visions,
Even on my servants, both men and women,
   I will pour out my Spirit in those days.
I will show wonders in the heavens
and on the earth,
   blood and fire and billows of smoke.
The sun will be turned to darkness
   and the moon to blood
   before the coming of the great and dreadful day of the
   LORD.
And everyone who calls
   on the name of the LORD will be saved" (Joel 2:28–32).

Because evangelism is such a threat, Satan will do anything he can to prevent, sidetrack, or discourage it. His anger and hatred mount when a caring Christian wants to witness to an unsaved friend or loved one. The Bible specifically warns us that Satan will try to obstruct any growth toward God's kingdom in the last days. He will use with renewed intensity the tactics he has always relied on.

People will mock Christian beliefs. "You must understand that in the last days scoffers will come, scoffing and following their own evil desires. They will say, 'Where is this "coming" he promised? Ever since our fathers died, everything goes on as it has since the beginning of creation'" (2 Peter 3:3–4).

Wicked behavior will continue. "The words are closed up and sealed until the time of the end. Many will be purified, made spotless and refined, but the wicked will continue to be wicked. None of the wicked will understand, but those who are wise will understand" (Dan. 12:9–10).

"But mark this: There will be terrible times in the last days" (2 Tim. 3:1).

There will be apostasy. "The Spirit clearly says that in later times some will abandon the faith and follow deceiving spirits and things taught by demons" (1 Tim. 4:1).

"Watch out that you are not deceived" (Luke 21:8).

"Be careful, or your hearts will be weighed down with dissipation, drunkenness and the anxieties of life, and that day will close on you unexpectedly like a trap" (Luke 21:34).

There will be political upheaval and great distress in the world. "Nation will rise against nation, and kingdom against kingdom. There will be great earthquakes, famines and pestilences in various places, and fearful events and great signs from heaven" (Luke 21:10–11).

False Christs will deceive many people. "Watch out that no one deceives you. Many will come in my name claiming, 'I am he,' and will deceive many" (Mark 13:5–6).

Not all Christians have the gift of the evangelist, but all are to evangelize. Every Christian is to be a witness for Christ. Satan would like church members to think that this is only the responsibility of pastors and church leaders. Satan would like us to think that "someone else will do it," but we might be the most effective communicator of the gospel in a particular situation. Friends and neighbors know us and how we live. The enemy will try to persuade us that we are not worthy; he will remind us of our failures; he will tell us that our witness will not make a difference. There is no question that Satan will escalate his all-out attack on evangelism.

The Attack on Church Attendance

EVEN THOUGH THERE SEEMS to be tremendous growth in the church worldwide, church attendance in the United States is at a standstill. While there seem to be pockets of "revival" and church growth, overall the American church has plateaued or is declining in numbers. According to Bill Hendricks of the Dallas Morning News, the number of born-again Christians remains at 32 percent. Canadian sociologist Reginald Bibby has shown that fewer than 10 percent of those who join evangelical churches come from outside the evangelical community, and most of that 10 percent usually come from other churches or through intermarriage. The Barna Research Group states that church attendance currently is at its lowest point in the last decade—42 percent of the U.S. population attends on any given weekend—and those who attend do not do so as often as they did five years ago. The average adult attendance at weekend church services is 92 people, a 9.8 percent decline from 102 in 1993.[29]

Bible reading outside of church services has hit a new low in America. Just 31 percent say they read the Bible during the course of a typical week.

It could be that the enemy has targeted the American church because of its tremendous commitment to missions over the years. More missionaries and more money has been given for world evangelism from the United States than any other country since the beginning of the church. This kind of commitment is a tremendous threat to Satan's work.

Satan is against any Bible-believing church that seeks to glorify God. He does not want us to be consistent in our church attendance or to be involved in the ministries of the local church. He wants to distract us from the worship, fellowship, and service we experience there.

The Attack on Unity in the Church

ONE OF SATAN'S FAVORITE strategies is to "divide and conquer." If he can persuade church members to feud, bicker, slander, or speak against one another, he can paralyze the church's impact on a community.

The church comprises all true believers who have been redeemed by the blood of Jesus Christ. Some estimate that there are nearly two billion people worldwide who say they are Christian believers. The number is very likely not this high, because among this group are people who have severely erred in their doctrine or who practice sinful behavior that the Bible clearly condemns. For example, members of the so-called gay church rationalize that they were created as homosexuals and therefore God will accept them this way. But that is not part of the true church of Jesus Christ. In fact, it is a mockery of God's holy standards of living, a result of Satan's deceptions. There are many others in the visible church who are not "born again" and proclaim a message of compromise and unbelief. Only God knows how many people are true believers.

This "true church" is the greatest threat to Satan in this world. In *The Screwtape Letters,* C. S. Lewis illustrates this concern of Satan.

> One of the great allies, at present, is the Church itself. Do not misunderstand me. I do not mean the Church as we see her spread out through all time and space and rooted in eternity, terrible as an army with banners. That, I confess, is a spectacle which makes our boldest tempters uneasy. But fortunately it is quite invisible to these humans.[30]

The Bible admonishes us to *maintain* the unity of the church, not to create it. Christians expect attacks from the outside, but not

from within. We need to protect our unity in God's "true church."
The Bible instructs us numerous times on this theme.

> "Warn a divisive person once, and then warn him a second
> time. After that, have nothing to do with him" (Titus 3:10).
> "I urge you, brothers, to watch out for those who cause divi-
> sions and put obstacles in your way that are contrary to the
> teaching you have learned" (Rom. 16:17).
> "I appeal to you, brothers, in the name of our Lord Jesus
> Christ, that all of you agree with one another so that there
> may be no divisions among you and that you may be per-
> fectly united in mind and thought" (1 Cor. 1:10).
> "So that there should be no division in the body, but that its parts
> should have equal concern for each other" (1 Cor. 12:25).

The Attack on Prayer

WHEN WE DISCUSSED THE weapon of prayer in an earlier chapter,
we observed that Satan will do anything possible to keep people
from this activity. Paul instructed us to "pray in the Spirit on all
occasions with all kinds of prayers and requests. With this in mind,
be alert and always keep on praying for all the saints" (Eph. 6:18).

We need to pray. The enemy is on the attack against prayer
because he knows how powerful the Christian's prayers are. We
must pray for our loved ones. We must pray for our communities.
We must pray for our churches. We must pray for our cities and
our nation. We must pray for the leaders in government. An apathy toward prayer is nothing less than the a paralysis inspired by
Satan.

Prayer is the key that opens the way for God to do what he
wants to do. In America there is much to pray about. Ralph Reed
writes,

> We live in a country in which one out of every three chil-
> dren is born out of wedlock, one out of every two marriages
> ends in divorce, one out of every three pregnancies ends in

abortion, and one out of every four high school students drops out of school without graduating. We have 90 million functional illiterates in our society. Murder is the leading cause of death for African-American males aged eighteen to thirty-four, and a minority adolescent male living in our nation's capital has a higher likelihood of being killed than an American soldier did in Vietnam.[31]

A man we will call William was raised in church, but turned his back on God in favor of drugs and the occult. He was lured into homosexuality and, with the growing emptiness in his heart, became suicidal. An attempt to end his life didn't work. His involvement in witchcraft, New Age thinking, reckless promiscuity, drugs—all failed to resolve his search for meaning.

William decided to attend his parents' church one Sunday, but his purpose was to disrupt the services by calling on evil spirits. His plan didn't work.

The next night, out of curiosity, William returned to the church. Thoughts of suicide filled his mind. The speaker, a missionary named Steve Hill, wanted to meet the young man and began to walk toward him. William panicked. His drug-saturated mind told him he could climb the wall next to him and escape. When this didn't work, William began to run from the church. Steve caught him in the foyer, and a group of Christians gathered around the tormented young man and began praying for him.

Later that night, with family members praying, the intense warfare ended and William surrendered completely to God. That night he began a new life in Christ. He collected his crystals, witchcraft books, and rock CDs into a pile in the backyard and burned them. William was miraculously delivered from his drug addiction, homosexuality, and demon possession.

The family had almost lost William while he was in his old way of life. But they prayed. Many other people had given up on him, but his loved ones didn't. They loved William, and they knew God could help him if he would only let Him. Prayer changed William. Prayer can change many things: a bad marriage, a terrible situation, a society.

The Attack on God's Word

WHILE TRAVELING ON AN early flight to the West Coast, I decided to sit alone.[32] I put a few papers and books in the empty seat next to me. I noticed that there was a teenage girl sitting on the other side of the empty seat, but I did not think she would want to talk. I was hoping to catch a nap for about a half-hour. However, about five minutes after I closed my eyes, I sensed that someone was looking at me. I opened my eyes to find that the young girl had put my books on her seat and moved to the empty middle seat. She was watching me.

"Hello, how are you?" I greeted her. She said in an Eastern European accent that she was fine but would like to talk to me. I knew that my nap was over.

I asked her where she was from and about her family. She explained that she was an exchange student from Russia and was living in a little town near Springfield, Missouri. Curious about her religious upbringing in Russia, I asked, "Did you grow up in a family that believed in God?"

She said that her family knew there was a God but did not know who He was, and they could not freely seek Him or worship Him. She said that just a few weeks ago she had attended a Bible study at her American high school. Her face brightened and she smiled when she said she had become "born again" after hearing about Jesus Christ. She said she had never experienced anything like that in her life.

I smiled back and said that I also had received this same experience of becoming born again. When she heard that, she could not contain herself from talking more about her newfound faith.

After a few minutes, she asked me what I did for a living. When I told her I was a minister, she became even more excited and said she had some questions for me. I encouraged her to ask, and her first question was, "I know my experience with God is real, but can you tell me why the Bible is true?" I was glad to explain why the Bible is true and how she could rely on God for anything she might experience.[33]

There is an all-out war today over the accuracy and trustworthiness of the Bible. The Bible is the inspired, inerrant word of God. Paul wrote, "All Scripture is God-breathed and is useful for teaching, rebuking, correcting and training in righteousness, so that the man of God may be thoroughly equipped for every good work" (2 Tim. 3:16–17). David said, "The words of the LORD are flawless, like silver refined in a furnace of clay, purified seven times" (Ps. 12:6). He also said, "Your word, O LORD, is eternal; it stands firm in the heavens" (Ps. 119:89).

Satan would like people to doubt all or part of God's Word. If we doubt the accuracy of one portion, why not another? The enemy will do anything he can to discredit Scripture and cause people to question its validity and stay away from the Divine Library.

Battling for the Bible

IN A MAGAZINE ARTICLE, D. A. Carson wrote,

> ... the Jesus Seminar, a group of 74 scholars who have crowned the first six years of their work by publishing *The Five Gospels: The Search for the Authentic Words of Jesus* (Macmillan). In fact, fully 82 percent of what the canonical Gospels ascribe to Jesus is deemed inauthentic, and much of the remaining 18 percent is only doubtfully authentic. . . . They present papers, discuss texts, and then with self-conscious theatricality, vote on blocks of text (sometimes an entire section, sometimes as little as a word or two) using colored beads.

> Casting a red bead means that the scholar thinks Jesus said this or at least something very much like it. Pink signals less certainty about a saying's authenticity. Gray means that Jesus did not say this, but maybe something of his thought hides obscurely behind the passage. Black signifies that the

text comes from earlier or later sources, but cannot be credited to Jesus.[34]

Carson's appraisal states it best: "The Jesus Seminar is not so much a work of scholarship as a tract for the times." Throughout the ages, Satan has tried either to destroy the Bible or to destroy people's confidence that it is God's Word. That will never happen because God's Word is eternal. The critics of His Word are all eventually proven wrong.

The present-day attack of Satan is rigorous, and his strategy has been well planned, but the Christian's weapons are more powerful. We can resolve to stand for what is right and true, no matter what the cost, because we have an eternal reward that will never fade away.

Defending the Faith

DR. BOB MOOREHEAD, A pastor in Seattle, Washington, wrote this declaration of faith:

> I'm part of the fellowship of the unashamed. I have the Holy Spirit's power. The die has been cast. I have stepped over the line. The decision has been made . . . I'm a disciple of His. I won't look back, let up, slow down, back away, or be still. My past is redeemed, my present makes sense, my future is secure. I'm finished and done with low living, sight walking, smooth knees, colorless dreams, tamed visions, worldly talking, cheap giving, and dwarfed goals.
>
> I no longer need preeminence, prosperity, position, promotions, plaudits, or popularity. I don't have to be right, first, tops, recognized, praised, regarded, or rewarded. I now live by faith, lean on His presence, walk by patience, am uplifted by prayer and I labor with power.
>
> My face is set, my gait is fast, my goal is Heaven, my road is narrow, my way rough, my companions are few, my Guide reliable, my mission clear. I cannot be bought, compromised, detoured, lured away, turned back, deluded, or delayed. I will not flinch in the face of sacrifice, hesitate in the pres-

ence of the enemy, pander at the pool of popularity, or mean-
der in the maze of mediocrity.

I won't give up, shut up, let up, until I have stayed up,
stored up, prayed up, paid up, preached up for the cause of
Christ. I am a disciple of Jesus. I must go till He comes, give
till I drop, preach till all know, and work till He stops me.
And, when He comes for His own, He will have no problems
recognizing me . . . my banner will be clear![35]

May we all be this committed. It is time to make our stand.

Eleven ✦

The Rise of the Antichrist

Adolf Hitler was deeply involved in the occult. He consulted horoscopes and had an uncanny ability to influence and control people. He also established a Federal Commission for Occultism in the government of Nazi Germany.

"He has the stare of an insensitive psychopath," Hans Frank, Hitler's former lawyer, said. Frank confessed to the prison psychologist that in serving Hitler he had been "in league with the devil."[1]

In his book *The Spear of Destiny*, Trevor Ravenscroft reveals that Deitrich Eckart, one of the founders of the Nazi party, introduced Hitler to the occult.[2] Hitler then became a member of the powerful Thule Group in Germany, an occult society that included judges, lawyers, doctors, university professors, industrialists, surgeons, military men, and members of the nobility. The members of this secret society were Satanists who practiced the black arts and communicated with demons. Eckart was the reigning high priest. Hitler was the promised messiah, whose coming the mediums foretold. Initiation into the deeper mysteries of this powerful and widespread fellowship of occultists included committing atrocities as part of the ritual magic. Horrible rites opened Hitler's soul to possession by powerful demons.[3]

One secret goal of the Nazi party was to introduce a new religion that the world would *have* to recognize. Instead of using the sign of the cross, the swastika would become this religion's symbol of allegiance. Hitler would be the messiah, and demons would guide the destinies of mankind.[4]

In their goal to control the world, Hitler and the Nazi party came too close for comfort. They did not succeed because God did not permit it. But it was no accident that Satan made an all-out attempt to set up a one-world government through this evil dictator. Satan senses that his time is short, so we can anticipate other attempts to control this world through a political system, economic structure, war, or all of the above. Hitler and other dictators like him are forerunners of the coming world leader known in Scripture as the Antichrist (1 John 2:18).

Is the Antichrist Alive Today?

IT IS VERY POSSIBLE that the Antichrist is alive today.

When Jesus taught the disciples about the end times, he described what those last days would be like (see Matthew 24; Mark 13; Luke 21). According to His teaching, the indicators are in place for the Antichrist to come onto the scene. There has never been another time in history when the signs were so right as they are today. We could be the terminal generation for the church age, when the body of Christ will be raptured. Soon after the church is taken from the earth, the Antichrist will become the leader of the one-world government. He will have an assistant whom the Bible calls the false prophet, and this assistant will seek to promote total allegiance to the Satan-inspired leader. When these two people gain control of the one-world government, they will make Hitler look like child's play. Satan will finally have the ultimate man at his beck and call to do his work.

The irony is that most of the leaders of the nations will make it possible for this new system of government to take hold even though they should know better. The German philosopher Hegel said, "History teaches us that man learns nothing from history."

George Sweeting, chancellor of Moody Bible Institute, said,

The world is looking for a powerful leader—an international figure to offer practical solutions to the world's problems of war, suffering, hunger and pestilence. Weary of hollow promises, people want a tried and proven super-leader, a shining knight strong enough to guarantee peace.

In the world today, international leaders change with amazing speed. Looking back over the past ten years, we see that the roster of leaders who were in power ten years ago and still are today is incredibly short. They have been removed from power by resignation, assassination, revolution, and death, and often their power base crumbles with their passing. Those who succeed them often blur their predecessor's achievements and discredit his words; then they fall from power just as quickly.

It is into this kind of political atmosphere that the Antichrist will come. He will offer peace and prosperity, but ultimately he will threaten the very existence of civilization. His power will be so complete and evil that only Jesus Christ will be able to conquer him and free the world from his grip, thereby bringing down the curtain on the present age.[5]

Satan's Agenda

SATAN WANTS TO BECOME "like the Most High" (Isa. 14:14). This incredible self-deception and sickening pride have grown to the point where he actually believes he can dethrone the Creator God. Even though Satan was defeated in his original rebellion, he has continued to try to usurp God's authority. His end-time strategy is to use a man to control the world through a one-world government. As Satan entered into Judas, so he will enter into this man, whom the Bible calls "the beast." This man will attempt to carry out the "perfect will" of Satan. Just as there is one triune God who has existed for eternity as the Father, Son, and Holy Spirit—so Satan will once again try to counterfeit God by creating his own trinity: Satan, the Antichrist, and the False Prophet. The False Prophet will be to the Antichrist what the Holy Spirit is to Jesus. Satan desires to be worshiped openly by all people. In the same way that we worship God the Father through Jesus Christ, the

Antichrist will be the one through whom people will worship Satan.

Billy Graham writes,

> This person is not Satan, but will use every evil device of Satan to oppose the work of God. The apostle Paul uses the term "the man of lawlessness" or "the lawless one" to speak of this individual (2 Th. 2:3, 8). He will be the embodiment of evil, and will have great power to deceive those who choose to follow him. . . . The time will come, therefore, when someone who is totally opposed to Christ will achieve great influence. However, in the end, he will be defeated by Christ.[6]

Who Is the Antichrist?

THE WORD ANTICHRIST MEANS "one who stands against Christ." This person will be directed by Satan to oppose Jesus Christ and call into question His reality and authority. Jesus is the Anitchrist's greatest threat, and it against Him that he will make his greatest strike. But the Antichrist's attack will not be obvious—at first. He will be "a master of intrigue" (Dan. 8:23); he will use flattery and manipulation to win people's favor (Dan. 11:32); and he will be a more clever deceiver than any other human being who has ever lived. His ability to deceive comes from the one who created lies.

The Antichrist is also called "another horn"—a little horn (Dan. 7:8; 8:9); "king of Babylon" (Isa. 14:4); "the man of lawlessness" (2 Thess. 2:3); and "the beast" (Rev. 13:1). He will be the humanist's hero and the materialist's answer. He will bring great relief to the hedonists, who want pleasure and gratification without moral restraint. Like many political leaders today, he will care nothing for the Bible or its God-given truths—or at best will feign respect for the Bible to gain followers.

He will deceive people into accepting his rule by convincing everyone that he has the answers to the complex problems of the world. Then he will abuse his power and "will oppose and will exalt himself over everything that is called God or is worshiped, so that he sets himself up in God's temple, proclaiming himself to be God" (2 Thess. 2:4). Through this man, Satan will finally and publicly declare his motive toward mortal human beings.

The Antichrist's power will extend to every area of life and every part of the world. All nations will follow his directives in his dictatorship over the military, religious, political, and economic systems. He will deny that Jesus Christ came in the flesh (2 John 7). In doing this, he will say that the incarnation of Jesus as fully God yet fully man did not happen. He will hate Christians, stand against any biblical solutions to human problems, and turn the world against the people who will come to Christ after the rapture of the church. John Bunyan wrote, "Antichrist is so proud as to go before Christ; so humble as to pretend to come after him; and so audacious as to say that himself is he."[7]

Given the continual bombardment of occultic movies, videos, television programs, music, and games, it becomes easy for people to accept the validity of such phenomena. The supernatural is fascinating to people, and most do not see the incredible diabolical evil in occultic practices. There is no question that the Antichrist will be immersed in the occult and the supernatural. He will perform "counterfeit miracles, signs and wonders" (2 Thess. 2:9). His ability will surprise few, but impress masses. The stage is set for this kind of leader. People are hungry for demonstrations of power from leaders, no matter how wicked they might be.

In his book *There's a New World Coming*, Hal Lindsey quotes from a 1984 interview conducted by *U.S. News & World Report* with Keith Harary, an experimental psychologist and co-author of the book *The Mind Race: Understanding and Using Psychic Abilities:*

> The U.S. government is interested in psychic research and for more than a decade has been sponsoring a multimillion-dollar research program at SRI International, a West Coast think tank. Beyond that, I can't comment or speculate on Defense Department involvement in this field. I can say, however, that the Soviet Union is interested in psychic research. The Soviets take it very seriously at the highest lev-

els—no doubt about it. My co-author, Russell Targ, and I have visited their remote-viewing laboratory in Soviet Armenia, and it appears the Soviets are also pursuing their interest in the theoretical possibility of behavior manipulation from a distance.[8]

There is no question that God will continue to demonstrate His power through godly people with the evidence of powerful signs and wonders. He has continually done this throughout the history of the church. He is a God of miracles who heals, delivers from bondage, and most important, forgives and redeems sinners. Yet Jesus warned that many deceivers, false Christs, and wolves in sheep's clothing would be active in the last days (Matt. 7:15; 24:23–25). We must use discernment as to whether people who promote manifestations, signs, and miracles are being used of God or are part of that group of people who will deceive many. We should not be impressed by miracles, but impressed with Jesus Christ.

Many a naive Christian or searching non-Christian has been thrown off course by such diabolical people. We learned a long time ago to evaluate people's ministries by their fruit. Are they giving glory to Jesus Christ? Do these people seek to point others to Jesus or to themselves? Is what they are teaching biblical? Are these people humble before the Lord? Our mental alarm clocks should go off if these people are promoting extrabiblical teaching. If we ask these kinds of questions, God will help us discern right from wrong, and godliness from deception.

The world is ready as never before for that "son of perdition" (2 Thess. 2:3 KJV). If the church were raptured from this world today, the Antichrist would have welcome acceptance tomorrow.

The Characteristics of the Antichrist

SCRIPTURE DESCRIBES WHAT THE Antichrist will be like and what he will do.

He will be against God and anything sacred to God.
He will blaspheme God. It is prophesied that the Jews will rebuild

their temple in Jerusalem and restore temple worship. But after a short period of time—three and a half years—the Antichrist will turn on the Jew, seize the temple, and shut down all worship (see Matt. 24:15; Mark 13:14; 2 Thess. 2:4; 1 John 2:22; Rev. 13:5–6). He will then enter the holy of holies and declare himself to be God.

There is a growing hunger among the Jewish people to rebuild the temple. In his book *Beginning of the End,* John Hagee quotes an organization called the Temple Foundation:

> Today, at the Temple Institute in Jerusalem, Biblical prophecy is being fulfilled. Here, you can see something which has not been seen on the face of the earth for 2,000 years: In preparation for the Third Temple, the Temple Institute has created authentic Temple vessels and priestly garments according to Biblical specifications. This is an ongoing process, and to date over 60 sacred objects have been recreated from gold, silver and copper. These vessels are not models or replicas, but they are actually made according to all the complicated nuances and requirements of Biblical law. If the Holy Temple were to be rebuilt immediately, the Divine service could be resumed utilizing these vessels. . . .
>
> In addition to its work on the recreation of Temple vessels, the Institute is conducting a number of related research projects. These include importation of authentic Red Heifers to Israel, in preparation for the ritual purification detailed in Numbers 19. Other firsts include the identification and gathering together of all 11 ingredients of the incense offering, and the long and exhaustive research in identifying the stones of the High Priest's breastplate—the Urim and Thummim. There is even advanced work being done by technicians and architects, using sophisticated computer technology, to design actual blue-prints for the Third Temple.[9]

He will devise and offer a peace treaty to Israel and the Middle East. This peace treaty will temporarily calm the constant unrest in the Holy Land. It seems that the treaty will have a term of seven years, but the Antichrist will break it halfway through (Dan. 9:27).

He becomes empowered by Satan. We can conclude that Satan's religion becomes the Antichrist's religion. It has always been Satan's goal to become God, and therefore the Antichrist will be an atheist or believe that he is God (see 2 Thessalonians 2:9; Daniel 11:36–37). When he breaks the treaty, he will boldly seize the temple the Jews will have built; he will sit in the holy of holies and declare himself to be God. His brazen declaration will shock, anger, and offend the Jewish community, but it will only be another demonstration of his unbridled leadership style.

He will demonstrate hatred toward both Christians and Jews (Rev. 13:5–7). The seven-year tribulation period will see persecution and martyrdom as never before, especially toward the new Christians who have come to Christ after the rapture.[10] These Christians will refuse to take the mark of the beast and refuse to cooperate with his evil system of government. The Antichrist will hate them for that reason, but even more so simply because they love God. People who love Jesus will infuriate him, and he will do all he can to eradicate them. Likewise, the Antichrist will endeavor to destroy the Jews because God loves the Jews, and anything God loves, Satan hates.

He will be a popular political world leader (Rev. 13:7–8). The Antichrist will set up a one-world government and a new world order. In our day we hear the terms "one-world government" and "new world order" more and more frequently. John Hagee writes,

> After World War I, "the war to end all wars," President Woodrow Wilson crafted the League of Nations to uphold peace through a one-world government. Adolph Hitler told the German people he would bring a "new order" to Europe. . . . The communists of the former Soviet Union pledged to institute a new world order. . . . Now the United Nations want to establish a new world order![11]

As the leader of the world, the Antichrist will wage war continually as he tries to hold his one-world government together. The focus of activity will be the tiny country of Israel, and specifically

Jerusalem. This city will be trampled for three and a half years (Rev. 11:1–2). Israel will be the seat of the Antichrist's government. Since God loves the Jews and loves Israel, Satan will aim his attack at the place God loves.

He will come from a country in Europe (see Daniel 7–8). In somewhat complex terms, Daniel covers thousands of years of history as he prophesies that in the last days ten nations will emerge from the location of the old Roman Empire. Daniel explains that this "end time" empire will come from the fourth world empire that has risen and fallen—the four empires being Babylon, Medo-Persia, Greece, and Rome. The ten nations will organize a political allegiance and become a formidable world force. The Roman Empire included most of Western Europe. The Antichrist will rise to leadership from one of these ten countries of Europe.

Today the European Economic Union is in the final stages of selecting a common currency that can be used in all its member nations. It is forming a structure to enable people from one member country to work in another. It is becoming a global economic force that will offer stiff competition to the rest of the world. However, this alliance is more than economic. It is also a political union of a nature that Daniel prophesied thousands of years ago.

He will devise a cashless society in which every financial transaction will be monitored. This worldwide economic system will restrict anyone from buying or selling without a "mark" that signifies allegiance to the Antichrist. This cashless system will be readily accepted by the world because it will counteract robbery, credit card theft, poor credit ratings, and bad checks. The apostle John wrote, "He also forced everyone, small and great, rich and poor, free and slave, to receive a mark on his right hand or on his forehead, so that no one could buy or sell unless he had the mark" (Rev. 13:16–17). This economic system will be a means of exerting control over everyone and identifying those who refuse the mark.

It is conceivable that a cashless society could be established in a fairly short time. Electronic scanners have eliminated the need for writing checks at many American supermarkets, department stores, and gas stations. Many employers provide direct, electronic deposit of paychecks into the bank. A *Reader's Digest* article titled "Coming Soon: Electronic Money" claimed that "millions of Americans are already receiving their wages and salaries electronically via direct deposits."[12]

When the cashless system is fully implemented, a person will simply pass his or her hand over a scanner and the deduction from the bank account will occur automatically. If there is no money in the account, the person's credit will automatically be used to complete the transaction. Homes, cars, heat and electric bills, medical charges, food, clothing, emergency needs—everything will need to go through the cashless system. Bank of America has advertised the slogan, "The whole world welcomes world money." We already have the technology for the cashless society. Only God holds the Antichrist back.

Robert J. Samuelson wrote in *Newsweek* magazine that

> Every age has its illusions. Ours has been this fervent belief of the power of prosperity. Our pillars of faith are now crashing about us. We are discovering that we cannot, as we had once supposed, create prosperity at will. . . . Worse, we are learning that even great amounts of prosperity won't solve all our social problems. Our Good Society is disfigured by huge blemishes: entrenched poverty, persistent racial tension, the breakdown of the family, and staggering budget deficits. We are being rudely disabused of our vision of the future. The result is a deep crisis of spirit that fuels Americans' growing self-doubts, cynicism with politics, and confusion about our global role.[13]

Samelson's observations and concerns about America can be duplicated in nations world-wide. The Antichrist will take advantage of the confusion and crisis that people feel and offer a false hope. The world will buy into it.

He will demand that people worship him. People will say, "Who is like the beast? Who can make war against him?" (Rev.

13:4). "All inhabitants of the earth will worship the beast" (v. 8; see also vv. 11–15; Daniel 8:11). Anyone who refuses to worship an image of the Antichrist will be killed (Rev. 13:15). Many have thought Antiochus Epiphanes,[14] Mohammed, Hitler, or others could have been the Antichrist. These people had traits similar to the real person to come.

He will be healed of a fatal wound (Rev. 13:3). Perhaps someone will have tried to assassinate him ("wounded by the sword," v. 14). He will be healed of the wound, and the "whole world" will be astonished and follow him. Many will wonder, "Who is this man who has such miraculous power, and authority, such amazing charisma and intelligence and who seemingly cannot even be killed?"

His kingdom will have enormous wealth (Rev. 18). This city or empire, called "Bablyon the Great," will suddenly be destroyed under God's judgment during the tribulation (v. 8). People around the world will be shocked by its sudden destruction and grieve over its downfall. They will say, "Woe! Woe, O great city, O Babylon, city of power! In one hour your doom has come!" (v. 10).

The secular world church will be allowed to grow until it becomes a threat to the Antichrist. This world religion will comprise cults, various religions, and so-called Christian faiths that do not follow the true apostolic, New Testament doctrine. But the Antichrist will quickly destroy all religions that do not acknowledge him as God (Rev. 17). Religions other than Christianity and cultic movements have never been a threat to Satan. The people who adhere to false religious faith are still under his control. At various times in history, they have cooperated with Satan in that they have become "drunk with the blood of the saints, the blood of those who bore testimony to Jesus" (v. 6). Religions with totalitarian power have always been guilty of killing God's prophets and His saints.

He will be a military leader but will lose the war of Armageddon (2 Thess. 2:8; Rev. 16:16; 17:14; 19:17–21). Although the Antichrist will have power and abilities greater than any other human being has ever had, he will be quickly destroyed. "The Lord Jesus will overthrow with the breath of his mouth and destroy by the splendor of his coming" (2 Thess. 2:8). This man's abilities and satanic impowerment are as nothing to Jesus Christ. When his time is finished, the Antichrist will be removed in an instant. His arrogance will turn into panic in a split second, when he suddenly realizes who Jesus is and sees that he has absolutely no power over Him (see Revelation 19:11–20).

The Antichrist's Personality

THE ANTICHRIST WILL HAVE a magnetic, charismatic personality and will quickly win the favor of the nations of the world. Most will place their trust in him because of his ability to seize the moment, control the crowd, and speak with mastery. At the time he assumes leadership, nations will desperately look to him to bring them together under a system that will settle the economic crisis, the military tension, and eliminate famine, poverty, and epidemic illnesses. He will be full of ideas and strategies. Perhaps he will even have a peaceful solution to the unrest in Yugoslavia, Central Africa, or the Middle East.

A false peace will come over the world at the beginning of the Antichrist's rule. It won't be long, however, before his true motives will be revealed. Without apology, the Antichrist will quickly turn against people who pose a threat to him. To keep the world under control he will orchestrate the persecution and killing of millions, making the Holocaust look small by comparison. He will be the sociopath to end all sociopaths and a master intimidator.

Some have questioned whether one human being could exercise such ultimate control over the destiny of mankind. Many have thought that the world will not stand by and let a leader destroy millions of innocent people. However, history reveals that this type of leadership has existed before. Why can't it come to pass in even greater magnitude in the future?

In his book *Exploring the Future,* John Phillips writes,

Joseph Stalin ruled the Soviet Union for twenty-five ter-
ror-filled years. Genghis Khan and Ivan the Terrible were
novices compared with Stalin. . . . It is estimated that Stalin
killed ten million peasants in his drive to collectivize the
farms of Russia. An additional ten million Ukrainians vanished; another five million died of famine. Stalin's secret
police shot and hanged whole villages. Millions were forced
into slave-labor camps to build roads and canals, cut down
forests, open mines, and gather harvests.

Stalin killed at least a million members of his own com-
munist party and purged the leading generals and thirty
thousand officers from leadership of the Russian army. All
Red Army officers who had gained experience in the Spanish civil war were brought home and shot.

Stalin banished his wife's sister to a concentration camp
for writing her memoirs. During and after World War II he
supervised the disappearance of some three million Jews in
Russia, the Baltic states, and Soviet-controlled Poland. At
the time of his death he was planning the systematic exter-
mination of every Jew in the Soviet Union.[15]

Under the Antichrist's leadership many nations will once again
close their eyes to the destruction of millions of guiltless people.

Famines will increase, and pestilences such as AIDS and the
Eboli virus will become widespread. Natural disasters will happen
more than in any time in history. The world will seem out of control. Literally billions of people will die during the seven-year
period called the tribulation. The world will see human destruction such as has not been seen since the flood of Noah's day, yet
even the number who died then will not compare with the number who will die during this short period of time. The Antichrist
will become only more heartless and insensitive as the human devastation intensifies. His only concern will be world domination.

John Phillips explains,

The antichrist will be an attractive and charismatic figure, a genius, a demon-controlled, devil-taught charmer of
men. He will have answers to the horrendous problems of

mankind. He will be all things to all men: a political statesman, a social lion, a financial wizard, an intellectual giant, a
religious deceiver, a masterful orator, a gifted organizer. He
will be Satan's masterpiece of deception, the world's false
messiah. The masses will follow him with boundless enthu-
siasm and will readily enthrone him in their hearts as their
world's savior and god.[16]

The Antichrist will be clever. He will be a flatterer and have
unparalleled boldness (Dan. 8:23–25; 11:21). He will be full of
pride and arrogance, like the evil one he will serve (Isa. 14:12–
17). He will be a deceptive liar like no other. He will be a man
without integrity, but will have the ability to make masses of intelligent people think his integrity is impeccable.

He will invent his own laws and disregard any law he chooses,
as in his breaking of the covenant with Israel. He will be unbridled, out of control, illegal, and a law unto himself (2 Thess. 2:7–
8). "The man of sin" will be the incarnation of sin itself. He will try
to do what Satan has sought to do for thousands of years: make
himself equal to God.

This leader will pretend to accept all religions, including the
Jewish faith, Islam, Buddhism, and the counterfeits of Christianity, but eventually he will even turn on all these with intense
hatred and destruction. During this time many will realize that
Christianity is the true faith, however. Yet these new Christians
will not take the mark of the beast, and most will be martyred for
their faith in Jesus.

Ultimately, after a reign of only a few years, the Antichrist will
attempt to do battle with God at the war of Armageddon. That
war will be his end. He will not be destroyed by a gun or a bomb,
but by the second coming of Jesus Christ Himself (see Revelation
19:11–21).

Satan has tried over and over to bring a person into a position
of supreme authority over the earth, but God has never permitted
it. When the Antichrist is revealed, it will only be because God
has sovereignly allowed it to take place. At present there is a
restraining power over Satan's desire to introduce this man to the

world. When the church is raptured from the earth, the restraint will be removed.

William Barclay makes three helpful observations about this end-time leader:

> (i) There is a force of evil in the world. Even if he could not logically prove that there was a devil, many a man would say, "I know there is because I have met him." We hide our heads in the sand if we deny that there is an evil power at work.
>
> (ii) God is in control. Things may seem to be crashing to chaos but in some strange way even the chaos is in God's control.
>
> (iii) The ultimate triumph of God is sure. In the end nothing can stand against him. The Lawless One may have his day but there comes a time when God says, "Thus far and no farther." And so the great question is, "On what side are you? In the struggle at the heart of the universe are you for God—or Satan?"[17]

God will never be outsmarted by the devil. God knows exactly what the enemy of our soul is doing. God has been patient with mankind, wanting as many people as possible to come to salvation. Now that the time is short, the events are rapidly passing, and the scene has been set for the final chapter of history, before the tribulation. It could be that this man is waiting and being prepared even now for Satan's greatest attempt, to take over the people of this world.

Twelve ✦

Resisting Temptation

D ave was going to be married in just a few weeks. I was concerned how his new wife would react to the tremendous fear
that was haunting him.[1] Even though Dave lived in one of the
safest parts of the city, he went to bed almost every night wondering whether something terrible would happen to him.

"I have several locks on all of the doors going outside. I have
installed extra locks on all of the windows. I sleep with a loaded
shotgun next to me," he told me.

I said, "Dave, I believe that we need to protect ourselves, but
what you have described to me is more than protection. Whatever
is happening here is paralyzing your life." I had given Dave and his
fiancée a temperament analysis test and observed that his fear
indicator had almost gone off of the chart. "What is it that is making you so afraid?" I asked him. "You have a black belt in karate,
and you are a big person. You come from a solid Christian home.
Where's the fear coming from?"

Dave said, "I don't know. I think I live a normal life, I live in
a safe neighborhood, and I can't think of any experiences in my
life that would make me prone to this."

"You know that your new wife is going to sense your fear when
she moves into your home, don't you?"

"That concerns me. I'm not sure what to do." Dave responded.

I began asking Dave a series of questions because I suspected
that he was feeding his mind fearful things. "Dave, please tell me

what kind of television programs you watch, what videos you rent, and what kind of books you read for entertainment."

He paused, then said, "I really like the programs with a lot of killing, violence, and suspense. These are the kind of videos I rent and usually the kinds of books I read in my leisure time."

For the next thirty minutes or so, Dave and I talked about all of the specific storylines. There was no question that they were full of fear, and violence. I said, "Dave, do you want to overcome this fear that you suffer with? I believe you can, within a few weeks or months."

Dave immediately responded, "No question, absolutely! I need to get this thing under control before I get married."

I said, "I'm going to give you an assignment. I want to speak to you again in two weeks, but starting now, I want you to stop watching and reading anything that has to do with violence, killing, or fear. I want you to take the time you would have normally spent entertaining yourself with this kind of stuff, and instead, read your Bible, read good Christian books, and participate in wholesome activities." I watched Dave's face as I was giving him the plan. I knew he was with me, he was desperate for help. I added, "Please call me every two days and let me know how you're doing."

A couple of weeks later Dave came back to the office with a smile of success on his face. I said, "Dave, how's it going? Are you feeling any relief from your fear?"

He said, "It's amazing, I did everything you asked me to do. I haven't watched television, or videos, and have read no secular books—just the Bible, and some Christian books that I've wanted to read. I feel calmer, and I'm sleeping better at night. The intense fear is not there."

We sincerely enjoyed our conversation that day and I again assigned him to continue in the habit of feeding his mind good things. He continued to gain control over his unusual fear because he began to think about things that were healthy, pure, godly, and true.

Dave was frequently tempted to be full of fear and anxiety. When this happened he literally paralyzed his social life and his relaxation at home. He was often captive to thoughts that continued to ask him, "What if someone breaks into my home tonight?" Or, "I wonder if someone I know will be murdered in *that* way?" After he watched a violent television program late at night or fell asleep reading a book about murder or suspense, he was unable to get any rest.

Dave's temptation is not uncommon. If we continually feed our minds with negative things, we will be full of negative thoughts. What we read, watch, or listen to has a tremendous effect on our lives. Moreover, the devil is constantly watching for an opportunity to bring even more of the temptations we struggle with. He cannot discern our thoughts, but he can observe our behavior and hear our conversation. When the enemy notices that we have a weakness, he will always take advantage of it.

Jesus said, "Out of the heart come evil thoughts" (Matt. 15:19). The apostle Paul said we must "take captive every thought" (2 Cor. 10:5). How do we control our thoughts? How do we gain control over the temptations that the devil brings to us?

Paul offers the solution: "Whatever is true, whatever is noble, whatever is right, whatever is pure, whatever is lovely, whatever is admirable—if anything is excellent or praiseworthy—think about such things" (Phil. 4:8).

I grew up in farming country.[2] As a young boy I watched the farmers prepare the soil each spring for the seed they were going to plant. I often wondered why they had to spend so much time turning the soil and breaking it up. One day I realized that the answer for a good crop lies in the soil and the seed. If the dirt was rich, well prepared, and watered enough, it was ready to receive the seed. Getting the soil ready was half the battle. The next thing the farmer did was to give that "ready" soil the best seed he could afford, because good seed produces good crops. Bad seed produces bad crops. No matter how well he prepared the soil, if the farmer planted sick seed into the ground, it would not produce good crops.

Our minds are like the farmer's soil. In Christians, God has worked and reworked the soil. He has given us great potential for producing an excellent crop, but we must feed our soil excellent seed—the qualities that Paul commends. When we do this, we greatly limit the enemy's ability to bring temptation to us. If Satan were to bring a "seed of temptation" when our minds are not receptive, that thought will die. The tempting thought is not the sin—it's what we do with that thought. D. L. Moody said, "When Christians find themselves exposed to temptation they should pray to God to uphold them, and when they are tempted they should not be discouraged. It is not sin to be tempted; the sin is to fall into temptation."[3]

William Shakespeare said, "'Tis one thing to be tempted, Another thing to fall."[4]

Dr. James Dobson relates this experience with temptation:

> Shirley and I had been married just a few years when we had a minor fuss. It was no big deal, but we both were pretty agitated at the time. I got in the car and drove around for about an hour to cool off.
>
> When I was on the way home, a very attractive girl drove up beside me in her car and smiled. She was obviously flirting with me. Then she slowed down, looked back and turned onto a side street. I knew she was inviting me to follow her.
>
> I didn't take the bait. I just went on home and made up with Shirley. But I thought later about how vicious Satan had been to take advantage of the momentary conflict between us. The Scripture refers to the devil as "a roaring lion looking for someone to devour" (1 Peter 5:8). I can see how true that description really is. He knew his best opportunity to damage our marriage was during that hour or two when we were irritated with each other.[5]

Dr. Dobson's soil was not prepared to receive the enemy's temptation, and he immediately reacted in a godly way. Because of his personal Christian disciplines, his mind was full of purity, faithfulness, and truth.

Our responsibility as Christians is to keep the soil of our minds and spirit receptive to the seed of God's truth and ready to repel any seed of temptation that the enemy would try to plant.

Everyone faces temptation because as long as we live there is an enemy who wants to defeat us. C. S. Lewis said, "No one knows how bad he is until he has tried to be good. There is a silly idea about that good people don't know what temptation means."[6] Oswald Chambers suggests that in tempting Jesus, Satan was trying to put Him on the way to becoming King of the world and Savior of men in a way other than that predetermined by God (see Matthew 4:1–11).[7] The writer of Hebrews says of Jesus' temptation, "Because he himself suffered when he was tempted, he is able to help those who are being tempted" (Heb. 2:18).

Satan has a unique strategy for every human being. He never plays fair. His evil forces keep an eye open for every opportunity to tempt us—when we have been involved in behavior that he knows will weaken our Christian faith, when we are emotionally depleted, mentally tired, or overwhelmed from battle fatigue.

In *Paradise Lost*, John Milton imagines a dialogue between Satan and his fallen angels over how they will influence human beings to join their conspiracy against God:

> . . . perhaps
> Some advantageous act may be achiev'd
> By sudden onset, either with Hell fire
> To waste his whole Creation, or possess
> All as our own, and drive as we were driven,
> The puny habitants, or if not drive,
> *Seduce them to our Party*, that their God
> May prove their foe, and with repenting hand
> Abolish his own works. This would surpass
> Common revenge, and interrupt his joy[8] (italics added).

The enemy would like nothing more than to persuade human beings, created in God's image, to yield to temptation and blame God for the punishment they receive as a result.

In a recent survey, pastors were asked, "When are you most likely to face temptation?" Their responses:

When I have not spent much time with God   81%

When I have not had enough rest   57%

When life is difficult 45%

During times of change   42%

After a significant spiritual victory   37%

When life is going smoothly 30%[9]

How Satan Tempts Us

ONE OF THE MOST striking accounts of temptation in the Bible is the story of David and Bathsheba. It is alarming because David was known for his love for God, but at this time in his life he had let his faith weaken. The Bible gives no indication that David had planned or anticipated an adulterous encounter prior to the night he saw Bathsheba.

> One evening David got up from his bed and walked around on the roof of the palace. From the roof he saw a woman bathing. The woman was very beautiful, and David sent someone to find out about her. The man said, "Isn't this Bathsheba, the daughter of Eliam and the wife of Uriah the Hittite?" Then David sent messengers to get her. She came to him, and he slept with her (2 Sam. 11:2–4).

Bathsheba became pregnant, so David plotted a cover-up through lies and deceit that eventually led to the murder of Uriah. It is a sickening story of how the enemy will carry our weaknesses to the furthest degree, if we let him.

The progression of David's sin went as follows. He was innocently taking a walk on the palace roof and undoubtedly surveying his capital city, Jerusalem. He noticed a woman bathing—still no problem. The sin began when David didn't turn his head and walk away. He watched the woman and began to think about her. When he was told who she was, the fact that she was married apparently didn't even phase him. David had probably already decided that he was going to "have" her.

After that night, David's life was never the same. God forgave him (2 Sam. 12:13), but his son was taken from him and he had to live with the memory, the embarrassment, and the shame. David had let God down. He hurt his family and did things he thought he would never do. We can imagine in David's mind he concluded a hundred times, "The small amount of time I spent in a lustful act was not worth the price I've had to pay for it."

Erwin W. Lutzer writes, "No matter how many pleasures Satan offers you, his ultimate intention is to ruin you. Your destruction is his highest priority."[10]

With us, there is a progression to temptation as there was with David. We see, talk about, or hear something. Then we linger over what we have just seen or heard. Our emotions become involved, and a desire grows. Next, we begin to meditate on this sinful behavior. Last, we plan a way to fulfill what we have been meditating on, and we satisfy the sinful desire in our hearts. James tells us, "Each one is tempted when, by his own evil desire, he is dragged away and enticed. Then, after desire has conceived it gives birth to sin; and sin, when it is full-grown, gives birth to death" (James 1:14–15).

Thomas à Kempis said,

> The process works like this. First, the thought is allowed to enter into our minds. Second, the imagination is sparked by the thought. Third, we feel a sense of pleasure at the fantasy, and we entertain it. Fourth and finally, we engage in the evil action, assenting to its urges. This is how, little by little, temptations gain entrance and overcome us if they are not resisted at the beginning. The longer we let them overcome us, the weaker we become, and the stronger the enemy against us.[11]

John H. Eastwood said, "People do not decide to be drunkards, drug addicts, prostitutes, murderers, or thieves, but they pitch their tent toward Sodom, and the powers of evil overcome them."[12] Had David turned his back and walked away when the temptation first came to his mind, his life would have been different. The second look trapped him.

The place to halt the process is at its beginning.

We cannot blame God when we fall into temptation. God is not the author of it. "When tempted, no one should say, 'God is tempting me.' For God cannot be tempted by evil, nor does he tempt anyone" (James 1:13). God may test us in order to strengthen our Christian walk, but He will never tempt us with sin. Our temptations come from two sources. Either they arise from what we have fed ourselves in the way of thoughts, behavior, communication, or observation, or Satan has arranged a trap when we least expect it.

In his commentary on James, William Barclay says:

> ... what is responsible for sin is man's own evil desire. Sin would be helpless if there was nothing in man to which it could appeal. Desire is something which can be nourished or stifled. A man can control and even, by the grace of God, eliminate it if he deals with it at once. But he can allow his thoughts to follow certain tracks, and his steps to take him into certain places and his eyes to linger on certain things; and so foment desire. He can so hand himself over to Christ and be so engaged on good things that there is no time or place left for evil desire. It is idle hands for which Satan finds mischief to do; it is the unexercised mind and the uncommitted heart which are vulnerable.
>
> If a man encourages desire long enough, there is an inevitable consequence. Desire becomes action.[13]

Thomas à Kempis said, "Temptations discover what we are."[14] An old proverb says, "He that lies with dogs rises with fleas."[15] How strong we are when a temptation comes depends on how well we have protected ourselves from the evil influences of this world. It's our choice.

We all have weaknesses, but times of temptation can serve to put us on the offense against them. We can decide to spend more time in prayer and deliberately do everything possible to counter that weakness. Erwin W. Lutzer said, "Temptation is not a sin; it is a call to battle."[16] If we go to the Lord in prayer when temptation seems overwhelming and, in turn, resist the temptation by walking away from it, we can feel assured that God will help us win.

Why Do Some People Give In?

OVER THE YEARS I have watched people rationalize certain behaviors that at one time they were "dead set against."[17] Something happened whereby they began to compromise. They began losing interest in daily Bible reading. They prayed less, began to miss church, and perhaps began to enjoy entertainments or activities they used to avoid. At times, when I am with such people, I can sense a wandering heart.

One evening my wife and I were having dinner with a prominent speaker who was visiting our city.[18] We took him to a restaurant that was known for its pleasant atmosphere. The waiters and waitresses sang to their customers, and there was a happy feeling in the place.

During the dinner conversation, we asked our friend about his wife and children. He quickly replied, "Oh, they're fine," then abruptly changed the subject.

He began talking about a recent visit to a beach in Europe where many people didn't wear bathing suits. He laughed and said, "We have these friends that love to go over there, so we go with them every year—to keep them company."

The other couple were Christians as well. I thought, *How could they go to this place?*

I asked, "Doesn't it offend you to go to that kind of beach?"

He was quick to respond, "No, it's all in fun. It's no big deal."

The subject of conversation changed again. Our friend mentioned how much money he was making on a new side business and asked whether we would like to get involved in it. There was nothing wrong with this business except that it had become the focus his life and was keeping him away from his wife and children.

My wife and I both noticed that he stared at several women in the restaurant and occasionally made suggestive comments about them. Throughout the evening we saw a side of our friend that we had not seen before. When we dropped him off at his hotel at the end of the evening, I said to my wife, "We need to pray for that man. If he doesn't change, his marriage will be over in five years and he might lose out with God."

Sad to say, my prediction proved right. He did divorce his wife within a few years. The couple with whom he took vacations to Europe are also divorced.

Our battle against temptation lasts for a lifetime. We cannot let down our guard. The armor of God must be in place day and night. Satan will watch and wait for a weak moment to strike. He is not in a hurry because he is only interested in the end result: our downfall. He doesn't make those who are already his uncomfortable. He is after those he doesn't have. He is gleeful when he can tempt Christians into doing something that will eventually cause their fall. The devil's incitement will be full of excitement and promise, but yielding to the temptation will bring us great shame, guilt, and embarrassment. When Adam and Eve sinned, they hid from God for the first time. They felt they just *had* to eat that forbidden fruit, and it became the most painful thing they had ever experienced.

The devil will offer different temptations for different seasons of life. Paul said, "Flee the evil desires of youth" (2 Tim. 2:22). New converts should not be leaders in the church because they "may become conceited and fall under the same judgment as the devil" (1 Tim. 3:6). Young widows have unique temptations that older widows might not face (1 Tim. 5:11). Every chapter of our lives will bring its own set of struggles. C. S. Lewis said, "The long, dull monotonous years of middle-aged prosperity or middle-aged adversity are excellent campaigning weather [for the devil]."[19]

When we begin to yield to temptation, things only become worse. We never quite find satisfaction, so the temptation demands more and more compromise. The alcoholic wants "only one more drink." The person who uses cocaine wants "just one more fix." The adulterer says, "Just one more night, to say goodbye." The pornographer thinks, "Just a brief look will not hurt anything." Alexander Maclaren said, "The temptation once yielded to gains power. The crack in the embankment which lets a drop or two ooze through is soon a hole which lets out the flood."[20]

Overcoming Temptation

WHEN ASKED HOW HE was able to overcome his drug addiction, Johnny Cash said,

> We prayed a lot.... I'm a free man now.... every once in a while I meet with a youngster who knows I used to be a drug addict, as he is now. He asks what he can do to kick the habit. I tell him what I've learned: "Give God's temple, your body, back to Him. The alternative is death."[21]

One of the most comforting verses in the Bible is 1 Corinthians 10:13. "No temptation has seized you except what is common to man. And God is faithful; he will not let you be tempted beyond what you can bear. But when you are tempted, he will also provide a way out so that you can stand up under it."

The apostle Paul assures us in this verse of several truths:

Our temptation is not unusual. Other people have experienced the same thing we have. We are not weird or different because we are going through a time of temptation. Many have gone before us, and many are suffering with the same problem. The devil likes us to think that our struggle is unique, because then we are weakened and lack the assurance that we can win. God has delivered—and is at present delivering—many people from the same temptation we are wrestling with, whether that is substance abuse, stealing, a bad temper, or sexual immorality. Do you feel all alone? You're not, and your temptation is not unusual.

God will not permit us to suffer more than we can bear. God knows what the devil is up to. He will not let the enemy give us more than we can endure. When we trust God with our lives one day at a time, He will continually bring us victory. If we are facing intense temptation, we have to hold steady: Keep praying, read the Bible, and attend a Bible-believing church. We can trust God one moment at a time and have the confidence that our loving heavenly Father will never let the pressure become more than we can handle. Sometimes people give up and say, "What's the use? This is the way I am!" But that is just another lie from Satan.

We are created in the image of God, and He will get us through. God did not create us to fail; He created us to be victorious and to spend eternity with Him in heaven.

Teen Challenge is a worldwide ministry that, in part, works with young people who are hooked on drugs. Its program has an extremely high success rate of helping people to get free and stay free of drugs. The governments of many countries have invited Teen Challenge in to help their people who struggle with drug addiction. The basic strategy of the program is to introduce addicts to Jesus Christ and then help them overcome their bondage one moment at a time. Often these desperate people become Christians because they have tried everything else and nothing has worked.

Teen Challenge workers understand that the addicts who become Christians have resources and abilities they never had before. Now Christ lives in them. At first the drug problem can seem overwhelming, and the person will feel like giving up. The Teen Challenge worker helps the person to understand that this will pass. Some recovering people are placed in halfway houses to be with others who have made it. Encouraged by these examples, they become stronger and more disciplined in not using drugs. By the end of the program, they know that God will not allow more temptation to come into their lives than they can bear. They realize that they can make it by trusting God one moment at a time. We must rest in that truth.

With every temptation, God will show us a way out. No matter what temptation comes to us, there is a way to overcome it and get away from it.

Joseph, the Hebrew young man sold into slavery by his brothers, was falsely accused for attempting to rape his master's wife. This accusation landed him in prison. His godly behavior and impeccable integrity cost him his freedom—temporarily.

The way of escape for Joseph was, at first, to refuse to even discuss the woman's invitation to sin. He repeatedly resisted her advances.

"With me in charge," he told her, "my master does not concern himself with anything in the house; everything he owns he has entrusted to my care. No one is greater in this house than I am. My master has withheld nothing from me except you, because you are his wife. How then could I do such a wicked thing and sin against God?" (Gen. 39:8–9).

There is no question that he did the right thing. We cannot negotiate when someone raises an idea that would be displeasing to God. But one day the woman confronted him in the house when there were no other servants around. "She caught him by his cloak and said, 'Come to bed with me!' But he left his cloak in her hand and ran out of the house" (v. 12).

When Joseph was backed into a corner by this person, he had no alternative but to run. He decided it would be better to suffer from offending his master's wife than from sinning against God. At this particular time in Joseph's life, his only reward for resisting sin was that he knew he was obedient to God. He could spend the rest of his life in prison—but he had peace in his heart.

God rewarded Joseph bountifully for his faithfulness. Two years later, the Pharaoh of Egypt needed someone to interpret his dream. No one could do it, except for Joseph, to whom God had given this ability. Through an amazing set of circumstances, Joseph was brought out of prison to interpret the Pharaoh's dream. With the interpretation, Joseph gave advice about what to do. The Pharaoh was so impressed with the wisdom of Joseph that he put him in charge of the whole land of Egypt. In a moment, Joseph was changed from prisoner to ruler.

God provided an escape for Joseph

—when he was sold into slavery.
—when an adulterous temptation came into his life.
—when he was falsely accused.
—when he was in prison.

No matter what came into his life, Joseph knew he could trust God. We can, too. In every temptation, there will always be a way out. We can choose the Christ-honoring course of action. We do not have to yield to temptation. God will not allow us to be backed into a corner where we have nowhere to turn. We can pray and ask God to show us the way out of our temptation.

Joseph Scriven had a life that many would describe as "filled with trouble." The night before their wedding, his bride-to-be drowned when she was thrown from a horse into a lake. He later began training as a military cadet, but poor health kept him from the career of his dreams. Scriven moved from Ireland to Canada and became a servant to the underprivileged, helping those who were physically handicapped and financially destitute. Tragedy came again when his second fiancée died of pneumonia not long after being baptized in a cold lake. It seemed that Joseph Scriven was destined to live alone and tolerate a career that was his second choice. For the rest of his life he experienced loneliness, meager pay for menial work, and physical illness.

Many people in Jospeh Scriven's circumstances would have turned bitter. We can imagine that he was tempted to become angry and disillusioned with life. Perhaps Satan spoke to him the way Job's wife talked to her husband when his life was falling apart: "Are you still holding on to your integrity? Curse God and die!" (Job 2:9). But like Job, Scriven didn't become resentful or angry. On the contrary, amid the tragedies, temptations, and trials, he wrote the beloved hymn "What a Friend We Have in Jesus."[22]

> What a Friend we have in Jesus,
> All our sins and griefs to bear!
>
> Have we trials and temptations?
> Is there trouble anywhere?
> We should never be discouraged—
> Take it to the Lord in prayer.
>
> In His arms He'll take and shield thee—
> Thou wilt find a solace there.

There is no question that in this life we will face trials and temptations. But God will help us through every one of them. It's our choice.

Thirteen +

Winning the Battle

E ven though Lisa grew up traveling with her father, Evangelist
Lowell Lundstrom, she wandered far from God. She ran away
from her ministry family into an insecure and dangerous world
filled with demonic strongholds. Struggling to survive, she did the
unthinkable and entered into a life of prostitution at age seventeen.

Years before, the devil had encouraged Lisa to become bitter
and resentful about her life. She became jealous of her brother
and sisters, especially their musical talents. Very few people knew
that inside Lisa was a growing pain and a spiritual downward spiral. This mental anguish would one day make her want to run from
everything she knew to be true and right. She thought, *I can make
it on my own. Life's not that difficult.* She was beautiful, intelligent, and sensitive and had a good personality—and the devil saw
an opportunity to destroy what was precious to God.

Lisa encountered many strange men during her nine years as
a prostitute. One night she met a man who had a strangeness and
deviancy she couldn't figure out. They met at a bar, then went to
a secluded house. She soon understood why he acted so strange.
Sensing danger, she dashed for the door. He grabbed her, put a
knife across her neck, and ordered her to lie down on a plastic
garbage bag. He was a serial killer who had murdered eighteen
women. Lisa was destined to be number nineteen.

When Lisa came into the world, her loving mother had
wrapped her in a warm baby blanket. Now she was to leave this

world, filled with terror and wrapped in a cold garbage bag. For four hours the crazed man ran knives up and down her body. He was mentally preparing to take another life. His trancelike stare seemed to come from another world. Lisa knew that if she tried to escape, he would kill her quickly.

In that dark moment, Lisa remembered how to pray. Her memories took her back to her childhood, when she and her family ministered to others. Once upon a time, years before, she had known how to pray, too. Even though her behavior was completely opposite of what God wanted it to be, Lisa somehow knew that He would listen now. Deep within her heart she cried out to God. "O God, don't let me die like this. I don't want my family to learn it ended this way!"

For years, the Lundstroms had known of their daughter's plight. They were heartbroken, ashamed. They continually questioned what they could have done wrong—which simply means that the devil was working on them as well because he will take advantage of every heartache, mistake, and tragedy. They never stopped praying, believing, and demonstrating their love in every way possible. They were sickened with Lisa's behavior but in their hearts they longed for her return. They knew her life was at risk in that kind of lifestyle. As the family traveled from city to city in the evangelistic ministry, Lowell would read the obituary page in the newspaper, fearing to see his daughter's name. As he spoke to thousands of people across the United States and Canada, he would ask Christians to "pray for Lisa."

Even though Lowell and Connie didn't know what was happening that particular evening, they sensed that their daughter was in desperate need of help.

As Lisa watched the eyes of her assailant, she knew death was near. One slash of the steel blade would sever her jugular vein. She tried with all her strength to hold back panic and continued to cry out to God. She remembered the presence of the Holy Spirit that she had experienced as a child—and in this critical hour she began sensing His presence again. She felt the power of God entering the room and pushing back the demons of darkness. Slowly the killer began to change his mind about taking her life.

Suddenly a miracle happened. With no explanation, the killer let Lisa go. A few minutes later, instead of taking her life, he killed himself. God had heard the prayers from all over the nation on Lisa's behalf. And God had heard Lisa's prayers. He had never left her.

This near-death experience shook Lisa to the core of her being. She also knew beyond any doubt that God had intervened for her. Yet, in spite of this realization, she kept running from God, who kept reaching out to her. It took another six years for Lisa to reach the bottom.

Lisa knew she was approaching a point of no return. God used the birth of a nephew to reach Lisa's heart. She wanted to see the boy grow up. She wanted to be an aunt he could be proud of. So this newborn baby rekindled a tenderness in Lisa's heart. This softening enabled her to rededicate her life to God.

Even though it was difficult to think about calling her mother and father, Lisa knew they would do whatever they could to help her. She called and said she wanted to come home. As she hoped, her mother and father forgave her immediately. Lowell dropped everything and drove two thousand miles—nonstop from Manitoba, Canada, to Houston, Texas—to be reunited with his precious daughter. Lisa's surrender to the love of her family led to her complete surrender to the lordship of Jesus Christ.

Now several years have passed. Lisa speaks regularly to young people about the dangers of running away from home and the heartache that rebellion will bring. Drawing on her experience, Lisa says, "Sin will take you further than you've ever been, make you stay longer than you ever intended, and soon you're doing things you never dreamed you would do.[1]

We must never forget that the devil "comes only to steal and kill and destroy," but that Jesus came to give life "to the full" (see John 10:10). There is no situation under the control of the enemy of our souls that our loving God cannot take back. We might think that it's too late for God to help us—that He's mad at us because of our behavior, or our problems are too big and have gone on for to long. Because the devil is a deceiver and a master at intimidation, he would like us to think that God can't or won't help. But Satan been defeated, and Christ can help.

God's Love: The Secret of Victory

THERE ARE THREE THINGS we must understand about God's love before we can feel confident of Christ's victory over Satan in our lives.

We can't earn God's love. It doesn't matter how good we try to be, how many times we go to church, how much we put in the offering plate, how often we read the Bible, or how much we pray—we cannot earn God's love. He loves us with an everlasting love. We cannot "work up" more love or acceptance. He is committed to us and will not give up on us.

We might say, "Well, I know that God loves Billy Graham or people like D. L. Moody or Susannah Wesley or the great men and women in the Bible. But He will never love me that way." Not true! God loves us in the same way He has loved every one of the men and women we admire and respect. God has no special people—only unique roles for ordinary people in His kingdom.

The playing field is level for all of us. "All of us have become like one who is unclean, and all of our righteous acts are like filthy rags" (Isa. 64:6). We all have a sinful nature and therefore need to be forgiven. God has provided a way for this to happen through the death, burial, and resurrection of His Son, Jesus Christ.

At one of Billy Graham's crusades, I was talking to him behind the platform before it was time for him to go out to preach to the waiting crowd.[2] As we conversed, I asked him a question I had wondered about for years. I said, "Billy, everywhere you go in the world to preach, tens of thousands of people come to hear you. How does this make you feel?" I could have anticipated his answer. Without hesitation, the evangelist replied, "It makes me feel like a worm." I think I knew what he meant. He was saying, It doesn't matter how many times I preach, or how many people want to hear what I have to say—my righteousness and my works are like "filthy rags."

Both our salvation and the divine help we receive to defeat the enemy are love gifts from God. "For it is by grace you have been saved, through faith—and this not from yourselves, it is the gift of God—not by works, so that no one can boast" (Eph. 2:8–9). We can't clean ourselves up or defeat the enemy in our own strength. We have to trust Jesus. We can't earn more grace or favor from God. We need only to have confidence in what He has already done for us. R. P. C. Hanson said, "Grace means the free, unmerited, unexpected love of God, and all the benefits, delights, and comforts which flow from it. It means that while we were yet sinners and enemies we have been treated as sons and heirs."[3]

Perhaps you grew up in a home where you were abused or you had a father who rejected you. Sometimes parents put unreasonable pressure on their children to achieve perfection in athletics or on the report card—and thus make acceptance conditional. Perhaps our brothers or sisters were continually putting us down. It may be that people we wanted as friends spurned us and treated us cruelly. There are also many single-parent homes today in which children feel an emptiness in their hearts because they have not received one parent's blessing. For any of these reasons we might have felt rejected our whole childhood and yearned for someone to say, "I'm proud of you. You're doing great! I love you!"

Listen: God does not reject us. He loves us with an everlasting love. He will forgive us of anything we have done. He will protect us from the enemies of the soul. And all these blessings are free. All this is called grace. We only need to receive His love and trust Him to protect us.

God has given me places of leadership that I never anticipated or sought.[4] He has given me the opportunity to lead thousands of ministers and millions of members in a church fellowship. I don't deserve this, and I am not good enough for it; however, I humbly accept whatever the will of God is for my life. I understand that the devil would like to attack me and bring me down, but I am not afraid of the devil because of God's incredible love for me. He will protect me, and I can rest in that. We all can. He will be the Father who says, "I love you and I am proud of you!" He will be the friend who wants to spend time with you. He will be the mother who will hold you in His arms. He will be your defender when the devil himself attacks. We cannot earn this love. We just receive it. Martin Luther said,

> "I believe in God the Father Almighty, Maker of heaven and earth." What does this mean? I believe that God has made me and all creatures; that he has given and still preserves to me my body and soul, eyes, ears, and all my members, my reason and all my senses; also clothing and shoes, meat and drink, house and home, wife and child, land, cattle and all my goods; that he richly and daily provides me with all that I need for this body and life, protects me against all danger and guards and keeps me from all evil; and all this purely out of fatherly, divine, goodness and mercy, without merit or worthiness in me; for all of which I am in duty bound to thank and praise, to serve and obey him.[5]

When the enemy attacks with temptation or trials, Jesus will be with us. Jesus said, "In this world you will have trouble. But take heart! I have overcome the world" (John 16:33). To put this another way, Know that as long as you live in this world, there will be trouble and trials; but be confident and take courage because Jesus Christ, who lives in you, has overcome this world.

Isaiah saw God's abiding presence when he reminded Israel that the Lord would never leave them:

> This is what the LORD says—
>   he who created you, O Jacob,
>   he who formed you, O Israel:
> "Fear not, for I have redeemed you;
>   I have called you by name; you are mine.

> When you pass through the waters,
>   I will be with you;
> and when you pass through the rivers,
>   they will not sweep over you.
> When you walk through the fire,
>   you will not be burned;
>   the flames will not set you ablaze" (Isa. 43:1–2).

Isaiah was reminding Israel that God would be their defender and their protector—not only physically, but mentally and spiritually, also. When the devil came against them, to bring discouragement or to overwhelm them, God would be there to help.

Three God-fearing Hebrew men were thrown into a blazing furnace because they refused to compromise their faith. When King Nebuchadnezzar watched the fire in the furnace, he said, "Look! I see four men walking around in the fire, unbound and unharmed, and the fourth looks like a son of the gods" (Dan. 3:25). The fourth man was Jesus! Not a hair on the heads of the Hebrew men was singed, and they didn't even have the smell of smoke on their clothing when they came out of the furnace.

In this world we will face rivers of trials and fires of temptation, but we will not face them alone. Jesus will stand with us. The river will not drown us, nor the fire burn us, if we trust God. Oswald Chambers said, "It is not our trust that keeps us, but the God in whom we trust who keeps us."[6]

When we feel that the temptation is too strong and we are about to give in, we must remember that Jesus will not permit more than we can handle. We can trust Him to get us through another day. When the devil knocks at our door with fear and anxiety, we can ask Jesus to answer the door!

No one knows what kinds of trials life might bring, but we can know that no matter what life brings, God will get us through it. Hold steady. Don't quit! The fire will not burn us.

We are a delight to God. In Psalm 18, David rejoiced because of the protection that God had given him. David said,

> He reached down from on high and took hold of me;

he drew me out of deep waters.
He rescued me from my powerful enemy,
      from my foes, who were too strong for me.
They confronted me in the day of my disaster,
      but the LORD was my support.
He brought me out into a spacious place;
      he rescued me because he delighted in me (vv. 16–19, italics mine).

David was literally being chased around the countryside by King Saul, who was jealous of him and wanted him dead. Numerous times Saul had tried to kill him, but David always found a way of escape. Saul put a price on David's head, causing him to live a life on the run, sleeping in caves, using rocks for pillows and the earth for his mattress. David said,

In my distress I called to the LORD;
      I cried to my God for help.
From his temple he heard my voice;
      my cry came before him into his ears (v. 6).

Saul was only a puppet in the hand of the devil. The enemy of David's soul wanted him out of the way. Satan was using Saul to attack David because he knew that if a godly king ruled Israel, it would ruin the devil's work.
      David said,

The cords of death entangled me;
      the torrents of destruction overwhelmed me.
The cords of the grave coiled around me;
      the snares of death confronted me (vv. 4–5).

But God delivered David, who reveals the amazing answer: "Because he delighted in me" (v. 19).
      Can we say, "God delights in me?" He does, and He is ready to show us that. Do we need help getting free from the claws of the devil? Does lust sicken yet entice and control us? Is our trial putting more and more pressure on our mind? Are our emotions on constant edge? Do we feel that we are becoming weaker spir-

itually instead of stronger? God delights in you! You are the reason He sent His Son to die. His love is everlasting. The enemy of our souls has limited power. He is no match for Jesus.

About God's love, Billy Graham said,

> Young people talk a lot about love. Most of their songs are about love.... "The supreme happiness of life," Victor Hugo said long ago, "is the conviction that we are loved." "Love is the first requirement for mental health," declared Sigmund Freud. The Bible teaches that "God is love" and that God loves you. To realize that is of paramount importance. Nothing else matters so much. And loving you, God has wonderful plans for your life. Who else could plan and guide your life so well?[7]

John Newton wrote, "If the Lord be with us, we have no cause of fear. His eye is upon us, His arm over us, His ear to our prayer—His grace sufficient, His promise unchangeable."[8]

Years ago, Mark and Huldah Buntain felt that God was asking them to go to Calcutta, India. They had been in the city and had seen the devastation that the devil can bring to millions of people. The poverty, the sickness, and the misery in Calcutta were—and still are—beyond description. Mark was a successful evangelist from Canada, and he didn't have to go to the other side of the world to find a successful career. But the tug in Mark and Huldah's hearts would not go away. So they, with their baby, Bonnie, went to Calcutta and began their work with a one-year commitment. One year turned into two, two turned into three, and then they knew this was to be a lifelong ministry.

As the years went by, the mission station grew. The now dynamic church was reaching hundreds with the gospel. Mark and Huldah started other churches and helped find national pastors for these congregations. They began a daily feeding program for women and children. All of these endeavors demonstrated the love of God to thousands.

Then Mark's health began to fail. He was exhausted. His nerves were on edge, and daily he fought a mental battle. The enemy, who had controlled that city for centuries, was not going

to let Mark destroy his work. Satan wanted to see the total ruin
and downfall of the Buntains' work in Calcutta. Mark hit bottom
emotionally, and out of his depression he said to Huldah, "God
has forsaken me."

Mark left Calcutta and sought help in another part of India.
After months of trying to get well, he realized that these people
had no answers for him. He left the hospital and went to "Childers
Lodge," a retreat center in the mountains of India. While walking
on the grounds one day, another missionary introduced himself to
Mark. He said, "Mark, many of us have been praying for you. We
heard of the difficulty you're going through." Mark didn't want to
talk to anyone and turned from the man and walked away. The
man called after Mark, "Mark, I've been where you are!"

With those few words, Mark knew that this man would have
some answers. He turned around, and for several days the man
was able to counsel and encourage him. Moreover, hundreds of
people were praying for Mark. Mark's nightmare began to end.
For the first time in months, he started feeling stronger and once
again sensed God's loving presence. The depression was over. He
returned to Calcutta with a new understanding of both the enemies' attack and God's power to heal and protect.

Wiser and stronger now, Mark and Huldah pressed on with
their work in Calcutta. Mark turned from the defense to the
offense, and over the next two decades God helped them build
the congregation to several thousand people. In addition, about
fifty other churches were started around the city. A system of
Christian schools was started and grew to ten thousand students.
A multi-story hospital was built that daily provided care for hundreds of the needy people. The daily feeding lines grew to more
than twenty thousand women and children. Numerous other ministries began in that city. Truly, what the devil wanted to destroy,
God protected. After Mark died, Huldah continued the work in
Calcutta, which flourishes to this day.

The devil will seek to weaken our faith and make us discouraged. We may be ready to give up on family members or even
marriage. Temptations might seem too big to handle. Perhaps our

problems have been with us for years. But we can hold on and be assured of God's help because He delights in us.

The Battle Is Almost Over

SATAN KNOWS THAT THE greatest entity that can counter his plan and strategies is the church of Jesus Christ. Once the church is removed from the earth, Satan will have tremendous liberty to quickly organize the nations of the world for the great battle called Armageddon. In his book *Angels*, Billy Graham writes,

> Lucifer, our archenemy, controls one of the most powerful and well-oiled war machines in the universe. He controls principalities, powers and dominions. Every nation, city, village and individual has felt the hot breath of his evil power. He is already gathering the nations of the world for the last great battle in the war against Christ—Armageddon.[9]

Even though Satan is certain that he will ultimately win, his days are numbered. God has an angel who will seize the devil at the end of the war of Armageddon and bind him for a thousand years (Rev. 20:1–3). When the thousand years are over, Satan will be temporarily released and once again try to marshal the nations against a holy God and His people. This attempt will be Satan's last. He will be thrown into the "lake of burning sulfur . . . . and will be tormented day and night for ever and ever" (Rev. 20:10).

The battle of Armageddon could be very near, and if that is the case, our personal battle with the devil is almost over. Christians are on the winning side. We have a relationship with God whereby we have discernment and an awareness of God's power and protection.

Feeling Surrounded

ELISHA WAS ONCE IN a situation that looked hopeless. He and his assistant were in the city of Dothan, and the king of Aram wanted him captured. The king sent horses and chariots and a strong force of soldiers to surround the city and find Elisha. Overnight the troops gathered, and in the morning Elisha's servant saw the forces on the hilltops. He panicked and ran to his master.

> "Oh, my lord, what will we do?"
>
> "Don't be afraid," the prophet answered. "Those who are with us are more than those who are with them."
>
> And Elisha prayed, "O LORD, open his eyes so he may see." Then the LORD opened the servant's eyes, and he looked and saw the hills full of horses and chariots of fire all around Elisha (2 Kings 6:16–17).

God had also surrounded the city. Aram's forces were no match for these invisible forces. God had sent his "chariots of fire," full of angels. The Puritan preacher Increase Mather wrote in *Angelographia*,

> Angels both good and bad have a greater influence on this world than men are generally aware of. We ought to admire the grace of God toward us sinful creatures in that He hath appointed His holy angels to guard us against the mischiefs of wicked spirits who are always intending our hurt both to our bodies and our souls.[10]

We may feel surrounded at times by the enemy of the soul. David Wilkerson said,

> The devil is not merely some cosmic jester or jokester, plotting and playing tricks on us just to make things difficult for us. His demonic spirits are not just imps who go around making life miserable. No—Satan's purpose is much more serious than that! . . . His one goal is to raze us, cut us down and leave nothing more than a memory.[11]

The enemy desires to ruin every Christian and every Bible-believing church. But God has an army that can remove the enemies' troops in a moment. This army is ready to respond at God's beck and call. God's holy angels are poised and prepared to defend and protect us. Elisha's prayer for his servant is for us as well: "O LORD, open his eyes so he may see."

The Grams family had endured a sleepless night full of fear on that fateful July 28. They felt very much alone, thousands of miles from their home in the United States. Molotov cocktails were thrown into the part of town where they lived. Machine guns and bombs went off throughout the night. The smell of smoke crept into their house from flames nearby. Shops, banks, and galleries were blown apart within yards of their home. Through the night they wondered whether they would survive.

Finally the night was over, and calm came to the community.

Almost two months later, Betty Jane Grams received a letter from a friend. She couldn't believe her eyes. The letter said, "I couldn't sleep last night. I kept seeing your faces and realized God wanted me to pray. So that's how I spent the night." The letter was written on July 28. The Grams family were once again reminded that God knew exactly where they were and what they were going through.[12]

In his book *Angels*, Billy Graham tells of a similar occasion.

It was a tragic night in the Chinese city. Bandits had surrounded the mission compound sheltering hundreds of women and children. On the previous night the missionary, Miss Monsen, had been put to bed with a bad attack of malaria, and now the tempter harassed with questions: "What will you do when the looters come here? When firing begins on this compound, what about those promises you have been trusting?" Miss Monsen prayed, "Lord, I have been teaching these young people all these years that Thy promises are true, and if they fail now, my mouth shall be forever closed; I must go home."

Throughout the next night she was up, ministering to frightened refugees, encouraging them to pray and to trust God to deliver them. Though fearful things happened all around, the bandits left the mission compound untouched.

In the morning, people from three different neighborhood families asked Miss Monsen, "Who were those four people, three sitting and one standing, quietly watching from the top of your house all night long?" When she told them that no one had been on the housetop, they refused to believe her, saying, "We saw them with our own eyes!" She then told them that God still sent angels to guard His children in their hour of danger.[13]

Staying Close to God

WE MUST ALWAYS REMEMBER that "those who are with us are more than those who are with them." The enemy will attack us, attempt to discourage us, tempt us, and accuse us. Even though he is a "roaring lion" looking for someone to devour, we are not to walk in fear or to live a life on the defense. We can walk in confidence and go on the offense. We have more than enough protection, and we have tremendous power in the Lord to defeat the enemy. The key is staying close to God.

When we stay close to Him, we have this promise: "Submit yourselves, then, to God. Resist the devil, and he will flee from you. Come near to God and he will come near to you" (James 4:7–8).

This is an assurance of great victory in spiritual warfare. We cannot defeat the devil or his demons in our own power. We cannot wash away the sins of our past or present. We cannot gain God's favor by doing good things. James is saying, "If you want victory over the devil, you must submit your life to God through His Son, Jesus Christ. There is no other way to win—if you want to overcome your guilt, bad habits, temptation, or the attack of Satan's invisible forces—you must submit and come near to God."

This formula might seem too easy. But that points up an amazing truth about the love of God. Many people—even theologians—have tried to make God's ways complicated, but God has made his plan of salvation and protection easy to understand. We simply have to give in to Him.

You might say, "How do I submit to God?" The answer is simply this:

Go to Him in prayer. Say, "God, I submit to you. I give my life to Jesus Christ. I believe that he died for me and rose from the dead. Help me live my life for your glory." God is with you right now. Whether you are in your home, on a park bench, in your car, in a prison cell—or even in a place where you know you should not be—He is ready to hear your prayer.

Decide to resist the devil. This means, decide to say no to his temptations. With the strength that God gives, you can decide to withstand and even oppose Satan's attack. You cannot do this in your own strength, but you can with the help of God. When the devil begins to tempt or accuse you, simply say; "I rebuke you in the name of Jesus" or, "I resist you and your temptations in Jesus' name." Then decide to not do what the devil is tempting you to do.

Years ago, I was going through a time where I knew the enemy was doing all he could to discourage me and slow me down from doing the will of God.[14] Even though I held steady, the battle seemed to intensify and I couldn't find relief. One day I began meditating on the goodness of God, and I decided to write the devil a letter letting him know that I would resist him, no matter what he threw at me. This letter brought great victory to me— and perhaps it will to you.

To the Devil:

You have called me weak—but the Word of God has said, "I can do everything through him who gives me strength."

You have said I can't possibly make a difference because I am only one—but the Bible teaches that God often uses one to shake the world.

You have said that preaching is foolish—but God says that by the foolishness of preaching God will change lives.

You have said that the Gospel of Jesus Christ isn't powerful enough to change people, but the Word says that the Gospel is the power of Almighty God for the salvation of everyone.

You have accused me, condemned me, tempted me and tried to discourage me.

But God tells me in His Word that:

I am holy	1 Pet. 2:9
I have no blemish	Col. 1:21, 22
I have no condemnation	Rom. 8:1, 31–39

I am a child of God	Jn. 1:12, Rom. 8:16, 17
I have the power of God within me	Eph. 1:19
I am blessed	Eph. 1:13
I am gifted	Eph. 4:17, 1 Pet. 4:10
I am loved of God	Jer. 31:3, Jn. 3:16

And by the way, I have decided to walk with my God of love and mercy, and to trust Him for all of my earthly life.

You have notice, that for me and my house, we will serve the Lord!

Very Sincerely,

Another reconciled-blood washed child of God!

_____

Signature

The letter was my way of resisting Satan's attack of discouragement. We all can do the same: "Resist the devil, and he will flee from you."

"Come near to God and he will come near to you." What James is saying here is not difficult to understand. God is ready to respond to any attempt on our part to come near to Him. We can pray in the yard. We can cry out to God when driving a car. We can quietly worship Jesus in our workplace. We can draw near to God anytime day or night. And when we draw near to God, our enemies will scatter. "May God arise, may his enemies be scattered" (Ps. 68:1). No matter where we are in life, we can decide to draw near to God.

Corrie ten Boom said, "There are two great forces at work in the world today: the unlimited power of God and the limited power of Satan."[15] Even though we might be in the battle of a lifetime, the hills and valleys around us are full of God's "chariots of fire." The enemies of our souls have been defeated, their abilities have been greatly limited, and the Battle has been won.

Notes ⨦

Chapter One—The Enemy of Our Souls

1. David Wilkerson, "You Are Precious to Him," Times Square Church Pulpit Series (Lindale, TX: World Challenge, n.d.), 3.

2. C. S. Lewis, *Screwtape Letters* (reprint, New York: Simon & Schuster/Touchstone Books, 1996), 15.

3. J. I. Packer, *God's Words: Studies of Key Bible Themes* (Downers Grove, IL: InterVarsity Press, 1981), 85–86.

4. Helmut Thielicke, "But Man Fell on Earth," *Christianity Today*, 4 March 1977, 15: adapted from a sermon collection, "How the World Began."

5. Mike Taliaferro, *The Lion Never Sleeps* (Woburn, MA: Discipleship Publications International, 1996), 40.

6. Lewis, *Screwtape Letters*, 37–38.

7. Edythe Draper, *Draper's Book of Quotations for the Christian World* (Wheaton, IL: Tyndale, 1992), 543.

8. Merrill F. Unger, *Demons in the World Today* (Wheaton, IL: Tyndale, 1971), 10.

9. Ed Murphy, *The Handbook for Spiritual Warfare* (Nashville: Thomas Nelson, 1992), 20.

10. Billy Graham, *Angels: God's Secret Agents* (Waco, TX: Word Books, 1975), 96.

11. J. Dwight Pentecost, *Your Adversary the Devil* (Grand Rapids: Zondervan, 1973), 272.

12. C. Fred Dickason, *Angels: Elect and Evil* (Chicago: Moody Press, 1975), 70.

13. C. S. Lewis, *Mere Christianity* (reprint, New York: Simon & Schuster/Touchstone, 1996), 109.

14. Graham, *Angels*, 98–99.

15. Draper, *Draper's Book of Quotations*, 150.

16. Ibid., 104.

Chapter Two—Unmasking the Evil One

1. This experience happened to Wayde I. Goodall while he was the pastor of a church in Auburn, Washington.

2. Billy Graham, *Angels: God's Secret Agents* (Dallas: Word Books, 1975), 105.

3. Edythe Draper, *Draper's Book of Quotations for the Christian World* (Wheaton, IL: Tyndale, 1992), 543.

4. Ibid., 149.

5. Ibid., 148.

6. Ibid., 150.

7. Helmut Thielicke, "But Man Fell on Earth," *Christianity Today*, 4 March 1977, 16.

8. Adapted from an article by Rich Wilkerson, *Enrichment Journal* (Fall 1995), 84.

9. Draper, *Draper's Book of Quotations*, 149.

10. C. S. Lewis, *Perelandra* (New York: Macmillan, 1944).

11. *Paradise Lost,* Book II, Line 44: quoted in Draper, *Draper's Book of Quotations,* 147.

12. William Barclay, *The Letters to the Galatians and Ephesians,* The Daily Study Bible (Philadelphia: Westminster Press, 1976), 99.

13. Draper, *Draper's Book of Quotations,* 148.

14. Whittaker Chambers, "The Devil," *Life,* 2 February 1948, 84–85.

15. George Sweeting, *Great Quotes and Illustrations* (Waco, TX: Word Books, 1985), 92.

16. Paul Enns, *The Moody Handbook of Theology* (Chicago: Moody Press 1989), 294–95.

17. Sweeting, *Great Quotes and Illustrations,* 92.

18. Draper, *Draper's Book of Quotations,* 150.

Chapter Three—The Forces of Darkness

1. Adapted from the *Pentecostal Evangel*, a publication of the Assemblies of God, 22 September 1996, 5.

2. W. E. Vine, *An Expository Dictionary of New Testament Words* (London: Oliphants, 1953), 114–17.

3. Walter A. Elwell, *The Concise Evangelical Dictionary of Theology* (Grand Rapids: Baker, 1991), 133.

4. Paul Enns, *The Moody Handbook of Theology* (Chicago: Moody Press, 1989), 298; see Merrill F. Unger, *Demons in the World Today* (Wheaton, IL: Tyndale, 1971), 102–8.

5. Charles C. Ryrie, *Study-Graph: Bible Doctrine II* (Chicago: Moody Press, 1965).

6. William Gurnall, *The Christian in Complete Armour* (Carlisle, PA: Banner of Truth Trust, 1986), 165–66.

7. David Wilkerson, *David Wilkerson Speaks Out* (Minneapolis: Bethany House, 1973).

8. Thomas E. Trask tells this story.

9. Paul relates a similar experience in Acts 16:16–18 during which he prayed in this way for a girl's deliverance from demons.

10. Hollywood celebrities—notably Shirley MacLaine and Linda Evans—have bought homes in the area, allegedly to be close to some of the New Age gurus who live there (*Valley Daily News*, Auburn, Washington, 23 July 1989, A6).

11. Ibid.

12. Ibid.

13. Ibid., A1.

14. Ibid.

15. Edward Murphy, *The Handbook for Spiritual Warfare* (Nashville: Thomas Nelson, 1992), 507.

16. David Yonggi Cho, *Church Growth* (Spring 1996), 4–5. Used by permission of Church Growth International, Yoido P.O. Box 7, Seoul, Korea.

Chapter Four—Satan's Plan of Attack

1. Some facts and details of this account have been changed to protect privacy and confidentiality.

2. James Patterson and Peter Kim, *The Day America Told the Truth* (New York: Plum Books, 1992), 204.

3. See 2 Corinthians 4:4. The unbeliever is blinded from seeing the light of Christ. When people become born again, their eyes become open to spiritual truth.

4. Edythe Draper, *Draper's Book of Quotations for the Christian World* (Wheaton, IL: Tyndale, 1992), 174.

5. Thomas E. Trask tells this story.

6. George Sweeting, *Special Sermons* (Chicago: Moody Press, 1985), 510.

7. See Ron Carlson and Ed Decker, *Fast Facts on False Teachings* (Eugene, OR: Harvest House, 1994). Christian Ministries International is based in Eden Prairie, Minnesota.

8. It is not unusual for people to remember keenly their departed loved ones in association with their places of residence, work locations, vacation spots, and so on. Often these locations bring back vivid memories—either pleasant or unpleasant. People who have these kinds of memories do well to be thankful for the enjoyable times and forgiving of the negative experiences.

9. This experience happened to Wayde I. Goodall while he was the pastor of a church in the Pacific Northwest. The names and some of the details have been changed to preserve privacy and confidentiality.

10. Sweeting, *Special Sermons,* 510.

11. Donald C. Stamps in *The Full Life Study Bible* (Grand Rapids: Zondervan, 1992), 1898.

Chapter Five—Assaulting the Church

1. Matthew Barnett is pastor of the Los Angeles International Church. Tommy Barnett oversees the work at this time.

2. *The Church Around the World* 26, no. 10: a newsletter published by Tyndale House, Carol Stream, Illinois.

3. Quoted by Kim A. Lawton, "The Suffering Church," *Christianity Today,* 15 July 1996, 56.

4. Ibid., 54.

5. *The Church Around the World* 26, no. 9.

6. Ibid., vol. 26, no. 10.

7. Lawson, "The Suffering Church," 54.

8. Haik Hovsepain Mehr, *Pentecostal Evangel,* 24 April 1994, 16.

9. W. Mark Bliss, *Pentecostal Evangel,* 24 April 1994, 17.

10. News Digest, *Pentecostal Evangel,* 22 March 1994, 24.

11. It was reported just recently that Mohammad Bagher Yusefi, a convert from Islam and an Assemblies of God pastor in Iran, was found hanged in a forest near his home city of Sari. He had raised two sons of Mehdi Dibaj while Dibaj was in prison for nine years.

12. Ed Decker and Ron Carlson, *Fast Facts on False Teachings* (Eugene, OR: Harvest House, 1994), 107.

13. Ibid.

14. List adapted from Decker and Carlson, *Fast Facts on False Teachings,* 10–12.

Chapter Six—Preparing for Battle

1. The pastor she referred to was formerly the pastor of a large church in that state. He had never met this young woman and lived about fifty miles from where these events happened. Pastor Miller did leave the church and became a key national and international Christian leader. There were no negative circumstances involved in his resigning from the church. Names and some details have been changed in this story to preserve privacy and confidentiality.

2. This experience happened to Wayde I. Goodall while leading a tour group of military personnel in Thailand.

3. Billy Graham, *Angels: God's Secret Agents* (Waco, TX: Word Books, 1975), 24.

4. Quoted by George Sweeting, *Great Quotes and Illustrations* (Waco, TX: Word Books, 1985), 252.

Chapter Seven—Our Victorious Conqueror

1. Ito Masashi, *The Emperor's Last Soldiers* (New York: Coward McCann, 1967), 148.

2. Ibid.

3. Ibid., 191.

4. Wayde I. Goodall tells this story.

5. David A. Noebel, *The Marxist Minstrels* (Tulsa: American Christian College Press, 1974), 103.

6. Eric Holmberg, *Hell's Bells: The Dangers of Rock'n Roll,* part 2 (Gainesville, FL: Real-to-Reel Ministries, 1989).

7. Ibid.

8. C. S. Lewis, *Mere Christianity* (reprint, New York: Simon & Schuster/Touchstone, 1996), 51.

9. George Sweeting, *Great Quotes and Illustrations* (Waco, TX: Word Books, 1985), 77.

10. Paul Lee Tan, *Encyclopedia of 7,700 Illustrations* (Rockville, MD: Assurance Publishers, 1984), 649.

11. Wayde I. Goodall tells this story. Details have been changed to protect privacy and confidentiality.

12. William Barclay, *The Letters to the Philippians, Colossians, and Thessalonians,* The Daily Study Bible (Philadelphia: Westminster Press, 1975), 142.

13. Sweeting, *Great Quotes and Illustrations,* 116.

14. Charles G. Finney, *Memoirs* (New York: Fleming H. Revell, 1903), 18.

15. Barclay, *Letters to the Philippians, Colossians, and Thessalonians,* 142.

16. Ibid., 143.

17. Sweeting, *Great Quotes and Illustrations,* 77.

18. Ibid.

19. Adapted from Richard Capen, *Finish Strong: Living the Values That Take You the Distance* (Grand Rapids: Zondervan, 1996), chap. 6.

20. Barclay, *Letters to the Philippians, Colossians, and Thessalonians,* 143.

21. James Dobson, *Focus on the Family Bulletin* 9, no. 5, June 1996.

22. E. K. Simpson, *Commentary on the Epistles to the Ephesians and the Colossians,* NICNT, ed. F. F. Bruce (reprint, Grand Rapids: Eerdmans, 1989), 191.

23. Chuck Colson, *Born Again* (Old Tappan, NJ: Fleming H. Revell/Spire Books, 1976), 57.

24. Tom Claus, *Native Discipleship in the Americas*, no. 8 (Phoenix: Chief, Inc., 1995), 10.

25. William J. Murray, *My Life Without God* (Nashville: Thomas Nelson, 1982), 14.

26. D. James Kennedy, *The Gates of Hell Shall Not Prevail* (Nashville: Thomas Nelson, 1996), 34–35.

27. Jeffrey C. Fenholt, *From Darkness to Light* (Tulsa: Harrison House, 1994).

28. Sy Rogers, "The Man in the Mirror," *Last Days Magazine* (1991), 2.

29. Stories of Nicky Cruz, Chuck Colson, William J. Murray, Jeff Fenhold, and Sy Rogers adapted from Kennedy, *The Gates of Hell Shall Not Prevail.*

30. Murray, *My Life Without God,* 239–40.

Chapter Eight—Our Invincible Armor

1. John Pollock, *The Man Who Shook the World* (Wheaton, IL: Victor Books, 1973), 238–39.

2. Pat Robertson, *Church Growth* (Spring 1996), 16. This is the magazine of Church Growth International, Seoul, Korea.

3. Ibid., 17.

4. William Barclay, *The Letters to the Galatians and Ephesians,* The Daily Study Bible (Philadelphia: Westminster Press, 1976), 182–83.

5. Hal Lindsey, *Combat Faith* (New York: Bantam Books, 1986), 184.

6. Ibid., 183.

7. David Wilkerson, "Perfect Righteousness," Times Square Church Pulpit Series, 19 August 1996 (Lindale, TX: World Challenge).

8. Lindsey, *Combat Faith,* 185.

9. Adapted from Scott Fontenot, *Mountain Movers Magazine* (October 1996), 10–11.

10. Barclay, *The Letters to the Galatians and Ephesians,* 183.

11. Edythe Draper, *Draper's Book of Quotations for the Christian World* (Wheaton, IL: Tyndale, 1992), 540.

12. Ibid., 185.

13. Ibid., 40.

14. This experience happened to Wayde I. Goodall.

15. Dwight L. Moody, *Notes from My Bible* (Chicago: Fleming H. Revell, 1895), 170.

Chapter Nine—The Arsenal of Prayer

1. Sue Burr, "Crushed in a Crowd," *Mountain Movers Magazine* (February 1994), 16–17.

2. Adapted from ibid.

3. J. Oswald Sanders, *Spiritual Leadership* (Chicago: Moody Press, 1989), 111–12.

4. Quoted in ibid.

5. George Sweeting, *Great Quotes and Illustrations* (Dallas: Word Books, 1985), 206.

6. Ibid., 206.

7. D. M. McIntyre, *The Prayer Life of Our Lord* (London: Morgan and Scott, n.d.), 30–31.

8. "Crows from Heaven," *Mountain Movers Magazine* (May 1996), 16–17. Adapted and used by permission.

9. Sanders, *Spiritual Leadership,* 111.

10. John Phillips, *Exploring the Book of Daniel* (Neptune, NJ: Loizeaux Brothers, 1990), 166.

11. E. M. Bounds, *Prayer and Praying Men* (London: Hodder and Stoughton, 1921): quoted in Sanders, *Spiritual Leadership*, 112, footnote.

12. Sanders, *Spiritual Leadership*, 205.

13. Ibid., 109.

14. Ralph Turnbull, *The Best of Dwight L. Moody* (Grand Rapids: Baker, 1991), 36.

15. David Wilkerson, *Have You Felt Like Giving Up Lately?*, Times Square Church Pulpit Series, 17 June 1996.

16. Ibid.

17. Division of Foreign Missions, *Moving Mountains* (Springfield, MO: Gospel Publishing House, n.d.), 19.

18. From a transcript of a taped interview with Frank Peretti by Jowell Kilpatrick, news editor, *Pentecostal Evangel,* for an article published 17 November 1996.

19. Adapted from Billy Graham, *Storm Warning* (Dallas: Word, 1992), 144–46. Used by permission.

20. This is the experience of Thomas E. Trask.

21. Adapted from Donald Stamps, "Power over Satan and Demons," *Full Life Study Bible* (Grand Rapids: Zondervan, 1992), 1487.

22. Thomas E. Trask and Wayde I. Goodall, *Back to the Word* (Springfield, MO: Gospel Publishing House, 1996), 98–99.

Chapter Ten—Satan's Present-day Strategies

1. Wayde I. Goodall tells this story.

2. Quoted in Kay Arthur, *Lord, Is It Warfare? Teach Me to Stand* (Portland, OR: Multnomah Press, 1977), 31.

3. H. B. London, *The Pastor's Weekly Briefing* from Focus on the Family, 25 October 1996.

4. Marguerite Shuster, *Power, Pathology, Paradox: The Dynamics of Good and Evil* (Grand Rapids: Zondervan, 1987), 135fn.

5. Ibid., 135.

6. Quoted in Bruce R. McConkie, *Mormon Doctrine* (Salt Lake City: Bookcraft, 1966), 321.

7. *The Barna Report,* January–February 1996.

8. In the book *The Future of the American Family* (Moody Press, 1993) the Barna Research Group provided data showing two important truths related to divorce. First, contrary to the media's myth about marriage, it is not true that half of all marriages end in divorce. That figure has been used by journalists for years, based on dividing the total number of divorces granted in a year divided by the number of marriages performed in that year. With about two and a half million marriages annually and about one and a quarter million divorces each year, the mathematics produce a statistic of roughly 50 percent. A more accurate way of determining what proportion of marriages dissolves is to figure out how many adults who have been married have also been through a divorce. On this basis, we found that about one out of every four marriages ends in divorce.

9. G. H. Pember, *Earth's Earliest Ages,* 13th ed. (London: Alfred Holness, n.d.), 382–83.

10. Donald E. Wildmon, "It Is Time to End the Religious Bigotry," *American Family Association Journal* (July 1995), 21.

11. *The Jerry Springer Show,* 8 May 1995: quoted in D. James Kennedy, *The Gates of Hell Shall Not Prevail* (Nashville: Thomas Nelson, 1996), 89.

12. "Network Programs Continue to Denigrate Christian Faith, Diminish Traditional Family, Promote Sexual Perversions," *American Family Association Journal* (February 1993), 5: quoted in Kennedy, *The Gates of Hell Shall Not Prevail,* 77.

13. Kennedy, *The Gates of Hell Shall Not Prevail,* 87.

14. S. Robert Lichter, Linda S. Lichter, and Stanley Rothman, *Prime Time: How TV Portrays American Culture* (Washington, DC: Regnery Publishing, 1994), 422: quoted in Kennedy, *The Gates of Hell Shall Not Prevail*, 87.

15. Mark Wingfield, "America Headed for Anarchy or Revival," Associated Baptist Press, 28 February 1996.

16. Ibid.

17. Larry Poland, newsletter of Mastermedia International Inc., 20 September 1990.

18. H. B. London, *The Pastor's Weekly Briefing* (25 October 1996).

19. The internet, with its pornographic possibilities, is a disturbing issue. Donn Rich Hughes, communications director of *Enough Is Enough*, an anti-pornography lobby based in Fairfax, Virginia, said, "The internet has become a central means for distributing pornography worldwide. Unfortunately, the worst and most deviant form of pornography has invaded our houses, offices, and schools via personal computer" (*Springfield* [MO] *News-Leader,* 5 June 1996, 1A).

20. Roseanne Arnold, *HBO Comedy Hour,* 20 June 1992: quoted in Kennedy, *The Gates of Hell Shall Not Prevail,* 88.

21. Bob Greene, "TV and Movies Teach Violence," *American Family Association Journal* (September 1993), 5.

22. Quote by Jim Talley, *Single Parent Magazine* (1996).

23. Wingfield, "America Headed for Anarchy or Revival."

24. Ralph Reed, *Politically Incorrect: The Emerging Faith Factor in American Politics* (Waco, TX: Word Books, 1994), 5.

25. Quoted in David Bryant, *The Hope at Hand: National and World Revival for the Twenty-first Century* (Grand Rapids: Baker, 1995), 27.

26. Kennedy, *The Gates of Hell Shall Not Prevail,* 7–8.

27. David Barrett, "The Growth of the Gospel!" *Mission Frontiers* 16 (July-August 1994), 5.

28. Ibid.

29. Trask and Goodall, *Back to the Word,* 82.

30. C. S. Lewis, *The Screwtape Letters* (reprint, New York: Macmillan, 1988), 12.

31. Reed, *Politically Incorrect,* 10: quoted in Kennedy, *The Gates of Hell Shall Not Prevail,* 232.

32. Wayde I. Goodall tells this story.

33. Trask and Goodall, *Back to the Word,* 10–11.

34. D. A. Carson, "Five Gospels, No Christ," *Christianity Today* (25 April 1994), 30.

35. Bob Moorehead, *Words Aptly Spoken* (Kirkland, WA: Overlake Christian Press, 1995), 99. © Dr. Bob Moorehead. Used by permission.

Chapter Eleven—The Rise of the Antichrist

1. G. M. Gilbet, *Nuremberg Diary* (New York: New American Library, 1947), 25.

2. Trevor Ravenscroft, *The Spear of Destiny* (New York: Bantam, 1974): quoted in John Phillips, *Exploring the Future: A Comprehensive Guide to Bible Prophecy* (Neptune, NJ: Loizeaux Brothers, 1992), 228.

3. Ibid.

4. Phillips, *Exploring the Future*, 228.

5. George Sweeting, *Great Quotes and Illustrations* (Waco, TX: Word Books, 1985), 17–18.

6. Billy Graham, *Answers to Life's Problems* (Dallas: Word Books, 1988), 301–2.

7. Sweeting, *Great Quotes and Illustrations*, 17.

8. Hal Lindsey, *There's a New World Coming* (Eugene, OR: Harvest House, 1984), 172.

9. John Hagee, *Beginning of the End* (Nashville: Thomas Nelson, 1996), 143.

10. The rapture is a future event described in 1 Thessalonians 4:13–17; Matthew 24:36–41; and in other passages of Scripture. At that time Jesus Christ will appear in the clouds and take all true Christians comprising the church from the earth to be with Him in heaven, leaving the rest of the world to endure without them during the period called the tribulation. Jesus' second coming, which will be recognized by all people, will occur after this time.

11. Hagee, *Beginning of the End*, 122.

12. Ibid., 120: quoting *Reader's Digest*, n.d.

13. *Newsweek*, 2 March 1992: quoted in Billy Graham, *Storm Warning* (Dallas: Word Books, 1992), 272.

14. William Blackstone wrote, "Antiochus was doubtless a type of Antichrist. And in his opposition to the worship of God, in his sacrifice of the hated swine in the temple and his merciless treatment of the Jews, he has given us a miniature picture of what the final Antichrist will do." Antiochus died long before Paul and John wrote of the future Antichrist (William Blackstone, *Jesus Is Coming* [reprint, Grand Rapids: Kregel, 1989], 110).

15. Phillips, *Exploring the Future*, 385.

16. Ibid., 277.

17. William Barclay, *The Letters to the Philippians, Colossians, and Thessalonians,* The Daily Study Bible (Philadelphia: Westminster Press, 1975), 213.

Chapter Twelve—Resisting Temptation

1. Wayde I. Goodall tells this story. Names and some details have been changed to preserve privacy and confidentiality.

2. This is the experience of Thomas E. Trask.

3. George Sweeting, *Great Quotes and Illustrations* (Waco, TX: Word Books, 1985), 246.

4. Edythe Draper, *Draper's Book of Quotations for the Christian World* (Wheaton, IL: Tyndale, 1992), 604.

5. James Dobson, *Focus on the Family Magazine* (May 1996), 5.

6. Sweeting, *Great Quotes and Illustrations,* 246.

7. Draper, *Draper's Book of Quotations,* 605.

8. John Milton, *Paradise Lost,* Book II, Lines 362–71 (New York: Mentor Books, 1981), 71.

9. Wayde I. Goodall, "Accountability, When a Pastor Needs a Pastor," *Enrichment* (Fall 1996), 79.

10. Draper, *Draper's Book of Quotations,* 605.

11. Quoted in Richard J. Foster and James Bryan Smith, *Devotional Classics* (San Francisco: Harper Collins, 1989), 85.

12. Draper, *Draper's Book of Quotations,* 605.

13. William Barclay, *The Letters of James and Peter,* The Daily Study Bible (Philadelphia: Westminster Press, 1976), 52–53.

14. Sweeting, *Great Quotes and Illustrations,* 245.

15. Draper, *Draper's Book of Quotations,* 605.

16. Ibid, 606.

17. This is the experience of Thomas E. Trask.

18. Wayde I. Goodall tells this story.

19. Sweeting, *Great Quotes and Illustrations,* 246.

20. Ibid.

21. Ibid., 245.

22. Adapted from Cliff Barrows and Billy Graham, *Crusade Hymn Stories* (Chicago: Hope Publishing, 1967), 40–41.

Chapter Thirteen—Winning the Battle

1. Story used by permission of Lisa Lundstrom, c/o Lowell Lundstrom Ministries, 1009 Sixteenth Street N.E., Wilmar, Minnesota 56201. Telephone: (320) 235–0222. Fax number: (320) 235–0548.

2. This is the experience of Wayde I. Goodall.

3. George Sweeting, *Great Quotes and Illustrations* (Waco, TX: Word Books, 1985), 133.

4. Thomas E. Trask is the general superintendent of the Assemblies of God.

5. Edythe Draper, *Draper's Book of Quotations for the Christian World* (Wheaton, IL: Tyndale, 1992), 271.

6. Ibid., 625.

7. Sweeting, *Great Quotes and Illustrations*, 177.

8. Ibid., 127.

9. Billy Graham, *Angels: God's Secret Agents* (Waco, TX: Word Books, 1995), 250–51.

10. Quoted in ibid., 253.

11. David Wilkerson, "The Nearness of God," 11 November 1996, Times Square Church Pulpit Series (Lindale, TX: World Challenge), 1.

12. Adapted from Betty Jane Grams, "The Night of the Molotov Bombs," *Moving Mountains* (Springfield, MO: Gospel Publishing House, n.d.), 43.

13. Al Bryant, *1,000 New Illustrations* (N.p: n.d.): quoted in Graham, *Angels*, 255–56.

14. This is the experience of Wayde I. Goodall.

15. Draper, *Draper's Book of Quotations*, 267.

SCRIPTURE INDEX ✦